Praise for DEREK R

EMERGE

"Derek explains fundamental knowledge and principles, known only to a few, in a way that will tantalize you, upend your current perspective, and send you in a new (and much more satisfying) direction." —**Bill Harris**, director, Centerpointe Research Institute

"This is one of those 'keep it with you and read it over and over again' books! Derek leads you on a journey into your soul—every step revealing more truth, more light, more love." —**Kristen Howe**, www.lawofattractionkey.com

"The Law of Emergence awakened me to my real identity and gave me the tools to cultivate a sense of inner peace, joy, and true happiness. It is the next stage of the soul's evolution." —**Amanda M.**, Starbucks executive

"We've been conducting business and creating under false assumptions. Derek challenges us to open up to a fresh worldview where we can work from our true nature, whole, abundant." —**Lindsay Crouse**, Oscar-nominated actress, *The Insider, Places in the Heart, The Verdict*

"I was on the verge of bankruptcy, about to lose my home and company. Derek's *Emergence* work helped me see and feel I had everything, and within 14 days, I had new customers and a lot of work. My banker hardly believed his eyes when he looked at my balance sheet!" —**Lars Rasmussen**, Denmark

"Derek guides you to discover what it is you really want...what you are really here for, so you can naturally create a life that is truly successful and ultimately satisfying." —**Brad Yates**, www.TapWithBrad.com

"Like the ancient sages and mystics who claimed that our true self is 'ever-free, ever-pure, and ever-wise,' Derek understands how to let your true nature emerge. Following his seven stages is a clear path to living in peace and joy." —**Paul R. Scheele, PhD**, CEO of Scheele Learning Systems, cofounder of Learning Strategies

"Derek Rydall lays out the spiritual truths that will help you transcend your limited beliefs, tap into your true power, and fulfill your higher purpose!"
—**Mark Harris**, producer of *Crash*(Academy Award for Best Picture)

"*Emergence* is a wake up call from your soul to let go to make room for all of the love, wealth, and health you desire and deserve because it's already on its way."
—**Christian Mickelsen**, author of *Get Clients Today*

"I was homeless and desperate. Now I'm in my own apartment, I'm engaged, my prescriptions have dwindled from 20-30 pills from different RX's, down to two pills a day, which are also disappearing. I am now a testimony to the very re-programming that Derek is sharing!" —**Jennifer**, Boise

"In *Emergence*, Derek Rydall gives us the answer to naturally creating a better life and discovering the breakthroughs that will provide us with success, abundance, happiness, and fulfillment." —**Dr. Joe Rubino**, creator of LifeOptimizationCoaching.com

"*Emergence* elegantly instructs and inspires us to listen deeply to the whisperings of life to discover how to bring forth our gifts in ways that touch those we care about, and furthers the evolution of love, service and goodness in our world."
—**Katherine Woodward Thomas**, author of *Calling in "The One"*

"A profound guide to enlightenment, *Emergence* is a beautiful reminder that we are not broken." —**Mark Porteous**, author of *Maximizing Your Human Experience*

"Derek reminds us that we are powerful beings who have forgotten our power!"
—**Leigh Taylor-Young**, Emmy award winning actress

"Derek Rydall's work is invaluable for any creative soul who wants to channel material the world is waiting for!" —**Dee Wallace**, healer, author, teacher, and actress (*E. T.*, *Cujo*)

"As a professional writer, I consider Derek's work one of the most valuable resources I have. It has been invaluable in helping me grow personally and believe in the possibility of what I create truly having a higher purpose."
—**Erik Bork**, two-time Emmy Award winning writer-producer of *Band of Brothers* and *From Here to the Moon*

EMERGENCE

SEVEN STEPS FOR RADICAL LIFE CHANGE

DEREK RYDALL

ATRIA PAPERBACK
New York London Toronto Sydney New Delhi

BEYOND WORDS
Hillsboro, Oregon

ATRIA PAPERBACK
A Division of Simon & Schuster, Inc.
1230 Avenue of the Americas
New York, NY 10020

BEYOND WORDS
20827 N.W. Cornell Road, Suite 500
Hillsboro, Oregon 97124-9808
503-531-8700 / 503-531-8773 fax
www.beyondword.com

Copyright © 2015 by Derek Rydall

Managing editor: Lindsay S. Brown
Editor: Anna Noak, Sylvia Spratt
Copyeditor: Sheila Ashdown
Proofreader: Jade Chan
Design: Devon Smith
Composition: William H. Brunson Typography Services

First Atria Paperback/Beyond Words trade paperback edition January 2015

ATRIA PAPERBACK and colophon are trademarks of Simon & Schuster, Inc. Beyond Words Publishing is an imprint of Simon & Schuster, Inc., and the Beyond Words logo is a registered trademark of Beyond Words Publishing, Inc.

For more information about special discounts for bulk purchases, please contact Simon & Schuster Special Sales at 1-866-506-1949 or business@simonandschuster.com.

The Simon & Schuster Speakers Bureau can bring authors to your live event. For more information or to book an event, contact the Simon & Schuster Speakers Bureau at 1-866-248-3049 or visit our website at www.simonspeakers.com.

Manufactured in the United States of America

10 9 8 7 6 5 4

Library of Congress Cataloging-in-Progress Data

Rydall, Derek,
    Emergence : seven steps for radical life change / Derek Rydall.
        pages   cm
    Includes bibliographical references.
    1. Self-actualization (Psychology).   I. Title.
    BF637.S4.R94   2015
    158.1—dc23
                                    2014024641

ISBN 978-1-58270-439-5
ISBN 978-1-4767-3160-5 (eBook)

The corporate mission of Beyond Words Publishing, Inc.: *Inspire to Integrity*

CONTENTS

THE SEVEN STAGES OF EMERGINEERING

FOREWORD

From the ideological halls of academia, the frontiers of scientific research, and the hallowed walls of houses of worship echo the theories of philosophers, scientists, spiritual teachers, agnostics, atheists, pundits, and pathfinders. On a global level you may also add to that list everyday people who are just as passionate about exploring the dynamics of human transformation, about diving into the depths of the evolutionary process and birthing their ultimate potential. Collectively, we ask the big questions about that which evolves the potentiality within galaxies and in you and me.

The theory of Emergence has a venerable history and has been debated at least since the time of Aristotle. In our twenty-first century, what is now called the Law of Emergence describes the architecture of the evolutionary process. Operative within the human being, it is the emergence of the ultimate state of consciousness that is our inborn birthright, which some call enlightenment, *satori*, *moksha*, or illumination. Imagine the planetary smile that would illuminate the spheres if the global family collectively came into harmony with the Law of Emergence. In truth, this is what has

viii FOREWORD

been happening since the big bang, which evolved from stardust to us, for as Carl Sagan wrote, "We are all made of star stuff."

So how does Emergence emerge? As organically as the oak tree emerges from the acorn seed when the conditions are right. While we do not cause the Law of Emergence to emerge in our lives, we do create the conditions by which it can. When consciousness is sufficiently fertile, the lotus flower of enlightened awareness blooms within us. This fertilization process is the spiritual technology Derek Rydall teaches in his seven stages for creating the right conditions for our "emergability" to be activated.

When, for example, you practice what Rydall calls "cultivating congruent conditions," a new way of relating and responding to inner and outer circumstances that occur on any given day appears on our mental, emotional, and spiritual menu. Instead of launching a volley of mental or verbal napalm on others or ourselves, compassionate patience and forgiveness become new options. He also shows us how to put an end to outer spiritual pretense and make our practice as applicable at the kitchen sink, driving on the freeway, walking our dog, or brushing our teeth as it is on the meditation cushion or yoga mat. Without hesitation, he makes it abundantly clear that we don't have to swap the joys of being human for the attainment of enlightenment and that we are already fine-tuned to serve the emergence of our inherently enlightened selves.

In the laboratory of his own consciousness and through conducting test-trials in his life, Rydall's Seven Stages of Emergineering provided him with factual evidence of their practical and transformative results. You may be confident that whether you are a new or experienced practitioner, the book you hold in your hands is a trustworthy guide to the glorious potentials seeking to emerge in, through, and as your life.

Michael Bernard Beckwith
Los Angeles, California

PREFACE

THE END OF
"SELF-IMPROVEMENT"

*What lies behind us and what lies before us
are tiny matters compared to what lies within us.*

RALPH WALDO EMERSON

They say the universe whispers in your ear, then taps you on the shoulder . . . and finally takes a two-by-four to your head.

I had to almost die twice before I got the hint.

I was broke, living in a one-room apartment, eating nineteen-cent boxes of mac 'n' cheese. I was heartbroken, the love of my life having left me for another man. And I was lost, with no idea where I was heading and no hope that things would ever change. But what made it all burn even more was that this was where I'd arrived *after several years of serious self-help therapy.* I'd worked hard to heal my past, love my inner child, and build my self-esteem, and yet I was so full of internal struggle and pain I could hardly cross a bridge without having to fight the urge to drive off it. whoa

You know you've found a dark place when the doctor says, "You're lucky to be alive," and you take that as *bad* news. I had nearly drunk myself to death the night before. Lying there in that emergency room, IV snaking out of my arm, the monitors telling me that I was, indeed, still among the living, all I could think about was, "How did this happen? How did all my efforts get me *here*?" After years of self-improvement, the only thing I had improved was my ability to describe why I was so screwed up. I had tried everything I knew; I had followed all the so-called expert advice. Was the problem that I just hadn't found the right path yet? Or was it just me? Was I broken beyond repair?

Most people who choose to heal or improve their life face this moment—this crisis point where they've done everything they're supposed to do and their life still isn't working. In these moments, when we've been knocked down yet again and are seriously considering whether we even want to get back up, we tend to ask these basic questions: Why? Why me? Why, when I've done everything right, is everything so wrong?

I know I asked those questions. A lot. Until I was given an answer that not only changed the way I saw my life but also made me see that I had been asking the wrong questions all along. The answer came in two parts, separated by a couple of years, like the cliffhanger of a television show leading to its shocking series finale. The storyline of my life, the character I had been playing, and the play I was in—all of it finally made sense.

The first part happened a short while after that night in the hospital, just when I started to stumble down what I thought was the "right" life path. I had become good at playing the role of a guy with his life together while inside I was still in pieces. But I was a struggling actor on the verge of a breakthrough, according to my agent, so there was no time to fall apart.

I loved acting. It allowed me to explore new ideas and inhabit new possibilities, giving me a temporary respite from whatever real pain I was feeling. And I was good at it. I thought it was my true purpose. And finally, after years of paying my dues, I landed a movie role that I believed was the start of something good for me, something that would lead to the life I was meant for.

I was right, but not at all in the way I'd imagined.

The shoot was troubled from the start. While the Jamaican location was beautiful, the script was not. And when the director and lead actress were fired, things started to unravel. Add to that some messy on-location romances and a general lack of creative fulfillment, and I was feeling restless. I needed to find something—anything—to be inspired by. So, during a break from shooting, I decided to do some late-afternoon snorkeling in a patch reef far from the shore of a secluded bay.

Swimming through the twining and twisting crests of elkhorn coral, sea fans, and finger coral, I followed some strikingly colored fish playing amidst sponges and anemones. For a moment, I imagined being one of them, free from the burdens of the life above. It was another world down there, almost mystical. And I wanted to lose myself in it.

Be careful what you wish for, right?

As I journeyed farther into this labyrinth, giving no thought to where I was, I actually did get lost. Really lost. I began frantically searching up and down the corridors of coral, trying to retrace my way, but the harder I tried, the more disoriented I became. *How stupid could I be?* I thought, my mind a storm of should-haves and if-onlys. I swam faster, my strokes angrier, as if somehow through sheer will I could break out of this underwater maze. Then, rounding a mass of coral that looked like a giant brain (something I seemed to be sorely lacking), I suddenly found myself stuck in a narrow pocket—fire coral surrounding me on all sides (the slightest contact of which would release the equivalent of hundreds of jellyfish stings) and rows of spiked coral below me, inches from my stomach, chest, and face. It looked like some booby-trapped tomb in an *Indiana Jones* movie. Only this was no movie set and I was no longer a cocky actor playing the hero. I was in real trouble, and I knew it.

I was barely able to use my hands to paddle and stay afloat. Lifting my head out of the water would've thrown my body off balance, skewering my neck and chest with the coral spikes. I could barely breathe in shallow, staccato gulps; a full breath would've pushed my chest and stomach straight into the spikes. The rapid breathing intensified my growing anxiety, creating a sort of euphoria that forced me to focus with every ounce of attention to keep from passing out. With the little room I had left for thinking, I ran through every possible scenario for escape for what felt like hours, imagining everything from being rescued by a passing fishing boat to washing ashore, blue-lipped, bloated, and bulgy-eyed, with a crowd of people standing around, shaking their heads, thinking, "What a shame," and the cast of my movie consoling each other as they grieved the tragic loss. I even managed to fantasize becoming a cover story in the Hollywood trades, mourning the untimely death of "such a promising actor."

Here I was on the verge of drowning, and my ego was still seeking its fifteen minutes!

But as the sun began to set and sand sharks began to weave through the twisting spiked coral below, my body became exhausted and my brain ran out of options as well as dramatic death scenes that would make me posthumously famous. I couldn't rationalize or fantasize my way out of this. All my (imagined) wit and charm were useless. All my coping and defense mechanisms—even all my positive thinking—were impotent. The curtain was finally pulled back on my mind, and, rather than being the master of the universe it proclaimed to be, it was exposed as nothing but a frightened little boy cowering at the controls, having no real power after all.

I was going to drown. And I *knew* it. My body had nothing left to keep me afloat, and without any way out, I simply had no more hope to hold on to.

All that remained was to surrender.

Not one of those "Dear God, if you get me out of this, I promise to go to church on Sunday" kind of surrenders. I had already tried to manipulate and negotiate my way out of this, and the universe wasn't bargaining.

There was nothing left but to let go.

So I did. *wow*

And in that moment—in that exact moment that I gave up, mentally and physically—a wave lifted me onto the one safe coral area that protruded out of the water. I was finally able to stand. And for the first time, I could see where I had gotten stuck.

The exit was inches from me all along.

But I saw something else. Looking into that reef, I realized that I had been swimming through a maze for years, following one brightly colored thing after another, looking for something to fulfill me, until I found myself trapped in such a confined sense of self that I was gasping for air, drowning inside. But in that space of complete surrender, in that moment when my mind reached the end of the tape, in that gap between thoughts, something snapped. My ego was ripped from its moorings. Humpty Dumpty fell off the wall. And amidst the broken shell, something else emerged. It was only for a split second, but it was enough to dramatically change my identity; that self-centered actor who went into that reef was not the guy who swam out.

But that was just the beginning of my swim through uncharted waters.

For the next several months, I was tormented by dreams of destruction and an inexplicable fear of death. The truth is I was dying. Not physically but egoically—and the ego doesn't know the difference between the death of an identity and literal death. And in the space this "death" created, I caught a glimpse of a Self that never dies, a Self that needs no improvement. For this actor, endlessly trying to fill a bottomless pit of inadequacy, it was like being freed from a prison I hadn't even realized I was in. Again, it was only a glimpse and I didn't have words to describe what I saw, but this time I got the message.

I dropped out of acting, limited contact with my family, canceled my cable service, and for the next few years spent all my time meditating, sitting at the feet of spiritual masters, immersing myself in the wisdom teachings of the ages, and seeking a deeper relationship with this Self that had swept me off my proverbial feet in my initial spiritual opening. I briefly studied to be a minister and then explored becoming a monk. But while fasting in one monastery, I became so hungry that I broke into the monks' kitchen in the middle of the night and stole food, so that pretty much ended my monastic career.

Ultimately, I became a licensed spiritual counselor at Agape International Spiritual Center, one of the country's largest transdenominational spiritual communities, under the mentorship of Michael Bernard Beckwith. Armed with the metaphysical principles of manifestation, I began teaching artists, media professionals, and seekers around the world how to actualize their full potential. A thriving consulting practice and a couple of published books later, things seemed to be going well. I was getting results. My clients were getting results. This stuff really worked!

Then I hit a wall.

Everything became more of a struggle. Techniques I'd used before were no longer working well. When I did "manifest" what I thought I wanted, there wasn't as much satisfaction. And in some cases, the more I tried to improve things, the worse they got. Not just for me but for countless others who were working with the latest success teachings. I persevered, but there was a rumbling beneath the surface.

Something was wrong with this picture. Something was missing. I tried doubling my efforts, but that just got me more stuck. Like pressing the gas pedal and the brakes at the same time, the tires were spinning but I wasn't moving. I had this creeping feeling that I had fallen back into that underwater maze again, but unsure of what I could do differently, I continued to teach. And shortly after that, during a talk I was giving, came breakthrough number two.

It was at a spiritual center in a suburban strip mall, sandwiched between a dry cleaner and a tanning salon. The audience listened attentively as I paced before them, speaking passionately about achieving their potential. I'd spoken on this topic many times, and by all objective standards I was on my game. But it was different that night. There was a tension in the air. The look on their faces wasn't one of inspiration; it was one of frustration. They'd heard it all before, tried it all before. And, despite my enthusiastic delivery, they weren't buying it.

I leaned forward, trying to verbally shake them out of their stupor, trying to infuse their hearts with the will to believe. But the harder I tried to inspire them, the more uninspired I was. I could feel the energy draining out of me as the words I spoke failed to ignite anything in them. Then something happened. I began to free-fall, but instead of hitting the ground, the ground opened up. Like a painted backdrop, my perception of reality parted. There was a moment of surprise, then expansion.

Then I saw it.

In essence, I could see that the whole model of personal development was wrong. We don't need to "attract" anything because we aren't lacking anything. We don't need to improve ourselves because the Self is already whole. Just as the oak is already in the acorn, everything we're meant to be and all we need to fulfill it is already in us—a perfect pattern and divine purpose. And, like the oak from the acorn, when the conditions are right, this innate potential naturally emerges.

This was the Law of Emergence.

With this profound shift in perspective, it was clear that our deepest desires are not something we have to go out and get; they're clues to what's inside us trying to get out. Rather than struggling to heal ourselves, our work is to strip away our false exterior and reveal our innate wholeness.

If we're already inherently complete, then all our efforts to fix, attract, or achieve something are—through the laws of deliberate creation—*exacerbating* our problems. This was why so many of our attempts to improve ourselves don't work or even make things worse. We attract a new partner but have the same old fights. We manifest a bigger paycheck and end up broke at a higher income bracket. Like trying to dig ourselves out of a hole, the harder we dig, the deeper we get. When we start from the false premise that we're broken or inadequate, no matter what technique we use or how sincere our efforts, it can *never* lead to true fulfillment but will keep us in a never-ending battle to improve a self that doesn't exist—except as a fictional concept in our head.

These were the missing links I had been searching for, the reason I, and so many others, had struggled to get lasting results—and the reason I had nearly killed myself trying.

As these insights burst into my awareness, I began to speak to my audience again: "The truth is, there's nothing wrong with you; you're not missing anything. *Everything you need to fulfill your destiny is within you, waiting to emerge*—and most of your efforts to achieve it are actually blocking it from happening! This is not another self-improvement technique. In fact, this is the end of the 'self-improvement' movement."

I was shocked by what I had just said. I had declared an end to the very thing I was trying to be a leader in. I had called my own bluff. But what I could suddenly see so clearly, shimmering before me like a highway in the desert, was a radical new path for real transformation, a path that encompassed everything we need to fully realize our potential and inhabit our lives. It may have been the end of self-improvement, but it was the beginning of something so much more.

To be clear, I wasn't saying it was the end of personal development—the natural process of developing our innate talents and capacities. I was saying it was the end of the illusion that we are broken, inadequate beings that must fix or add something to ourselves to be complete. I was saying it was the end of this compulsive pursuit to fill a perceived hole that has no bottom or reach for a bar that is as elusive as the ever-receding horizon line. I was saying that the whole way we'd learned to actualize our potential was *completely backward from how we were designed to grow.*

Worse than that, it was taking us further away from our true Self, the very source of everything we were seeking.

I quickly realized that if what I had discovered in the concept of Emergence was true (and was applied), there would soon be little need for self-help programs or gurus. Admittedly, this was not the most well-thought-out business strategy for an aspiring self-help guru. If my clients followed the Law of Emergence, I would eventually have no returning customers!

Of course, that's actually the intention of sincere teachers. Their goal is never to create followers but leaders—to give people back to themselves. From the framework of Emergence, it's no longer about being a sage on the stage but a guide on the side.[1] And in that light I realized there might still be a job for me after all. Just as it isn't the farmer's job to put the plant into the seed and make it grow but simply to cultivate the conditions that allow the seed and soil to do what they're naturally designed for, so, too, is the role of a practitioner of Emergence. I realized that this truth I had discovered acted as a law, like gravity. And like gravity, I didn't have to make it work; I just had to come into alignment with it—and help others do the same—and the law would do the heavy lifting.

That night, as I stood looking out at the audience, I knew the message of Emergence was exactly what they needed to hear. And what followed confirmed it: the audience breathed a collective sigh as if to say, "Free at last."

And just like that, the tension in the room was gone.

I closed my eyes and took a breath as well, letting it all sink in. And when I looked back out at the audience, they weren't the same. Instead of seeing people who needed to improve themselves, what I saw were perfect beings waiting to emerge. I felt like Michelangelo, who believed that God had already created everything and his job was only to set free the completed masterpiece imprisoned in the block of stone. Staring into the faces of those audience members, what I saw were divine masterpieces hidden in blocks of mortal stone. And I knew that from that day forward, my work was not to fix or change anyone but to help people set themselves free. *Amen*

With continuing economic stress, unemployment, and home loss, many of our external structures of security have been taken away. The wave of wealth-creation books promising instant riches—ironically followed by the biggest economic crash since the Great Depression—has left many seekers feeling disillusioned. Now more than ever, people are looking for an authentic way to stabilize their life and reclaim their freedom. Emergence will lead you to that solid ground, in the only place the world can never touch—within you. At a time when so many are feeling fearful and uprooted, Emergence will bring you home again, where you will find peace, inspiration, and the power to finally fulfill the purpose for which you were born.

This book is the culmination of teaching the principle of Emergence to tens of thousands of people around the world. My hope is that it will release you from the need to look outside for answers and authorities, from trying to fill up places you perceive to be empty or even from trying to "attract" things. On the pages of this book, I will share with you the secret of your real sovereignty and power; the ancient truth that great mystics have tried to teach but has been largely lost; a principle that great leaders in every field have employed to create masterpieces, build empires, and ignite revolutionary forces—and yet has rarely been understood or articulated.

Until now.

Together, let's bid good-bye to "self-improvement" and begin the process of setting our real Self free.

INTRODUCTION

THE RADICAL PATH HOME

We shall not cease from exploration, and the end of all
our exploring will be to arrive where we started and know
the place for the first time.

T. S. ELIOT

My friend gives directions to her home via an oak tree. She says, "You'll come to a curve in the road. Watch out for the rather large and unfortunate potholes. Next you'll see a school crossing, and then right past that is a huge oak tree. That's where I'm at. Just park underneath and come on in; the door is open."

Most of the world could give directions via oak trees. There are around six hundred types, both evergreen and deciduous. And like many large families, they've traveled far and settled everywhere. They can be found in cool climes and tropical latitudes. In fact, they live on every continent but Antarctica, unless you count the ships of old, made of oak, that sailed the treacherous seas to bring their treasures to that frozen landscape.[1]

The oak tree in front of my friend's home is well past a hundred years in age, which means its taproot has forged very deep, almost as deep as the thirty-foot height of the tree, with a trunk seven feet around, and a root system a third again the diameter of the tree's crown overhead. The deeply riveted bark has patches of smooth wood where it has been worn away by generations of weather and human hands touching the exposed heartwood, as if feeling for a pulse of connection.

This idea of connection seems apt, considering that oak trees used to be seen, symbolically, as a guardian of doors or the door itself—a door into the next season because it waxes and wanes as the seasons do—or the gateway between earth and heaven because it touches both the ground and sky. It was a door of hospitality, a portal that looks simultaneously into the past, the present, and the future.[2]

Beyond a doorway, it has also stood as a keeper of knowledge and laws. The oak provided teachings for the people of the old cultures. It told them about the forest and offered examples of flexibility and generosity in its wood (both green and hard), leaves, tannin, acorns, galls, and bark.[3] Those who held great wisdom were said to "know the oak."

It is no wonder, then, that humans have long sought to claim the attributes given to the oak in myth, culture, and history: strong, sustaining, reliable, majestic, and connected to the divine.

The oak in front of my friend's home is venerable. That's a good word for a wise old oak, for it has seen much, its character traced in the knurs, in twists and turns of the trunk, and in its branches that reach out and up so exuberantly. In its life, this centenarian has lived in a way to be admired. From acorn to grandfather tree, it transformed in an amazing—and, when you think about it, radical—shift from nut to green tree to mature, fully realized oak. It has lived each stage along the way wholly (and holy), never resisting the emerging impulse that first cracked its protective shell and forced it to die to its acorn identity, never shying away from the soil as its roots were driven into the dark so that its branches could rise toward the light, never fearing the droughts but instead digging to find its deeper resources, never fighting the storms but standing strong when able or bending instead of breaking, and never judging any stage as better or worse.

The oak has things to teach us about Emergence.

The Seed, the Soil, the Roots, the Fruits

While I'll be enlisting the help of other metaphors throughout this book to explain the principles and practices of Emergence, I've chosen to expand on the oak more than others. I could have picked many other trees. In one sense, the principles underlying all growth, from seed to root to flower and fruit, mirror the Emergence process. But it's tough to beat the elegance of the oak.

The great oak starts as an acorn, a small seed that we'd never expect to be able to bring forth such a mighty expression, capable of living for generations and providing food, shade, shelter, and so much more to hundreds of other creatures. Yet packed inside that seed is the invisible pattern perfectly designed to become the oak—and not only one oak but offspring that could become forests of oak spanning eons. Inside that almost miniscule piece of carbon material is an infinite, eternal potential.

The same is true for you.

Just as the acorn doesn't come here an empty shell and then set about "making something of itself," neither were you designed for such a thing. The seed you started as already contained the material and mechanics of its fulfillment—and the fulfillment of everyone and everything that evolves from your life.

Really think about the implications of that statement. Just as a single acorn contains endless forests, the seed of your being contains all the ideas, contributions, and impact your life will ever make—and the ripple effect your life has and will have on the world around you. All it takes is the right conditions for its emergence.

As the acorn grows, the roots dig down into the dark soil, the detritus of all the things that have outlived their usefulness and fallen into decay. Working with nature rather than against it, using what exists rather than resisting it, the conditions are cultivated for its emergence. When we embrace all the "dirt" of our lives, tapping into the raw experiences we've been planted in, surrounded by, and sometimes nearly buried under, the process of Emergence turns those dark, seemingly decayed parts into the nutrients that nourish new growth. We lose the struggle, judgment, and shame of a life spent trying to avoid, repress, or deny what is or has been and transmute everything into something useful and supportive. We establish deep roots, bring forth rich fruits, and evolve the way nature intended.

As the oak emerges, driving its roots deep and broad, its shoots rise up and out, reaching for the light. The deeper the roots go, the higher the branches can grow. The innate balance of nature understands that you can't have one without the other. If the tree strove for the light without grounding itself in the dark soil, it wouldn't be able to sustain its reach. A good drought would dry it out, a forest fire would burn it up, and a strong storm would topple it. Our human process of Emergence is the same. When we ignore our roots and focus only on our reach, we lose our center of gravity and our source of sustenance. When we aren't grounded in a deeper place, in something that nourishes us beneath the surface of our busy lives, we become easily parched, burned out, and knocked down by the winds of change.

But when we find our natural balance through the Emergence process, we're able to reach higher and wider than our little acorn-self had ever imagined—and often faster than expected. Just as the sapling has "flushes"—sudden growth spurts, sometimes several in a season—we, too, are capable of taking quantum leaps mentally, physically, spiritually, creatively, and in every other area of our life. The more rooted we are in the soil of our soul, the more connected we are with the seed of our true nature. And the more congruent we are between the two, the greater heights our life can scale.

Finally, the oak matures, providing shade and shelter and seeding the world with new acorns that become new trees. As we emerge into our full potential and activate our deepest purpose, the gifts we share create and support an ecosystem that allows our world to evolve and thrive.

This is the realization of the oak; it happens every time an acorn is allowed to emerge as nature had intended. When the conditions are right, nature always fulfills its promise. It can't do anything else. The acorn is whole, complete, and perfect in its acorn-ness, in part because there's always an oak waiting under its cap. Not a pine tree. Not an apple tree. But an oak tree. Every time. We know this to be true. We know it would be foolish to believe that the acorn should become something else. We would never expect that an acorn, no matter how much "pine tree training" it went through, would ever become a Christmas tree. And we wouldn't want it to. Everything fulfills its function, which in turn supports everything else in an ever-expanding, self-sustaining system.

This is also our realization as humans, if we are left to our natural course. Alas, we rarely have that luxury. The collective consciousness of separation, limitation, and self-preservation has created a false sense of self and a deep disconnect from the seed of our true nature. Rather than clearing away the debris that has gathered over the place we were planted and cultivating the soil of our soul, we have become lost in an attempt to become something other than what we truly are. Fortunately, the metaphor of the oak—of any naturally growing thing—holds true: as the acorn and its oakhood are perfect ideas that will always emerge when the conditions are right, so, too, will you.

Please let that sink in. This is not just more New Age gobbledygook, a feel-good affirmation, or an interesting theory; this is universal truth. There really is an underlying order we can lean on, depend on, and trust. We see it every day in nature all around us. It's an order that doesn't require us to make it happen but, as Michael Bernard Beckwith says, "to make it welcome."[4] The process of Emergence brings you back to this solid ground upon which your life can finally blossom into its full potential.

Why Emergence? Why Now?

With the availability of so many books and programs for improving our lives, fair questions would be, "Why Emergence? Why now?" I would follow that up with another question: "How are the other options working out?" Or to borrow a common question posed at the beginning of each US presidential election cycle, "Are you better off than you were four years ago?" And not just you but everyone else. While we've made great strides as a society, we're still hungry, broke, scared, and killing each other at alarming rates. And if we aren't killing each other, we're killing ourselves. In the United States, there are twice as many suicides as homicides.[5] And many more of us are just doing it slowly, through food, drugs, stress, or repression of our true heart's desires. The hit television program *The Walking Dead*, it turns out, is a reality show. We've become zombies, in a way, using all manner of quick fixes and distractions to numb us to the pain we're really feeling.

Now, before you reach for that bottle of Pinot Grigio to wash away these troubling facts, please understand that I'm not a skeptic. In fact, I sometimes drive people up the wall with my idealistic and romantic musings. But I also know you can't heal what you don't feel, and you can't get where you want to go until you're honest with where you are. It's like those signs in a mall that read, You Are Here; you need an accurate assessment of your starting point or you'll just end up wandering in aimless circles. But there's something else that happens when we get conscious—I mean, really conscious—about the state of things, without judgment, blame, or shame.

We start changing.

If we're not living consciously, our ego will use every trick in its playbook to keep us the same, all the while making us *think* we're changing, convincing us we can't, or just dulling our senses with another episode of *Here Comes Honey Boo Boo*. The ego's job is self-preservation, often at any cost, and real change is a threat to its system software. It's an evolutionary artifact that was designed to ensure that this experiment called humanity made it. And with billions on the planet, it worked. Unfortunately, it's now the very thing decreasing our chances of survival.

Let's face it: things aren't working the way we've been doing them. And no amount of doing more of the same, individually or collectively, will ever solve our problems. Please hear this: We will *never* solve our problems in any sustainable way doing things the way we've done them or being the people we've been. We must evolve. The only way to evolve is to go to a higher level. And the only way to go to a higher level is to access the evolutionary impulse beyond the conditioned mind and its endless tales of worry and woe—because the conditioned mind can only create another version of its current condition.

And how do you access (and even accelerate) this evolutionary impulse? Through the Law of Emergence and the process of Emergineering.

We've already covered why this is such a unique, even revolutionary path compared to what we've been taught, and this book is designed to give you a masterful ability to apply this revolutionary principle to every area of your life. But because the ego often resists any idea that could cause real change, asserting, "I already know this," "There's nothing new here," or simply, "I don't get it," and because an acceptance of the basic premise of the Law of Emergence is necessary for its successful application, let me spend a few more moments explaining what's different about this.

As stated before, the principle of Emergence reveals that everything we could ever need is already within us—*the exact opposite* of how most of us have been conditioned to live. When we believe that someone or something *outside* us is our source of security or supply, we struggle and strive, fight and die, and generally twist ourselves into pretzels trying to get what we think we don't have or hold on to what we've already got. The result is endless anxiety, resentment, burnout, and way too many trips to the fridge in the middle of the night, not to mention everything described earlier about our current state of affairs.

This conflict ends when you live the principle of Emergence in your life.

And then the real fun begins.

Imagine what your life could be like if you woke up every morning knowing and feeling that you held within you everything you could ever need. How would you interact with others? How much more open, generous, loving, and at peace would you be? If you knew that you held the design, mechanics, and power to create the life of your dreams within you, what new choices would you make? What bold actions might you take?

Emergence is *how you were designed to live.*

This is not an overstatement. It's what every great spiritual master or enlightened philosopher has expressed. It's how the whole universe is set up. It started with nothing and burst forth into everything. The big bang is the epitome of Emergence. And you, being the universe in miniature, are a mini big bang waiting to happen. You are an individualized expression of infinite perfection, the offspring of the divine. You possess the same creative ability as the creative intelligence of the cosmos.

If you're still doubtful, maybe a little uncomfortable with all this talk of purpose and potential, unsure of how to let this inherent power and beauty emerge, you are not alone. This, after all, is the journey we're about to embark on. A journey that will take you home again, where your oak already stands, tall and majestic, the guardian of your soul and the doorway to your greatest life. Maybe you've been walking a particular path for a long time, searching for a sign that you were getting close. Maybe you've walked many paths, finding nothing but rocky terrain, washed-out trails, and dead ends. Maybe you've stopped on the side of the road, feeling too weary to move on. Whatever twists and turns your travels have taken you on, the path has led you here.

To this book, this moment, this map.

A person who is true of heart and mind is said to have a "heart of oak." That thing you feel, that thing that has driven you to find your way over mountains, through storms, and across rough waters, that is your oak-heart, calling you home.

It's my greatest honor and privilege to join you on this liberating path back to your Self. Let's take a walk, shall we?

What's Inside

This book is broken into nine chapters, starting with "The Law of Emergence," which lays the spiritual, scientific, and philosophical foundation for reengaging with this ancient principle. By doing so, we will clarify the critical difference between attraction and Emergence, busting the myth of cause and effect and turning the outside-in world inside out again, clearing the field of your mind and heart to be freshly cultivated for Emergence. From there, you begin "The Seven Stages of Emergineering"—seven chapters that reframe the conventionally held concepts of self-actualization and manifestation within the new Emergence model and that guide you step-by-step through this revolutionary process of personal transformation.

In "Stage One: See the Completed Vision," you'll learn a unique excavation process for uncovering your true destiny—that seed of potential already planted in the soil of your soul.

aha!

In "Stage Two: Cultivate Congruent Conditions," you'll learn to bring your inner life into alignment with the vision, tuning the frequency of your mind, like a radio, to the station where your music is already playing, ending the struggle to make something *happen* and mastering the skill of making it *welcome*.

In "Stage Three: Create the Quantum Plan," you'll engineer the inner and outer vision into a way of life that takes you from living on accident to living on purpose.

aha

"Stage Four: Give What Appears Missing" reveals the real secret that whatever's missing is what we're not giving. We have an infinite storehouse of good locked up in our consciousness. In this chapter, you learn how to reverse the flow from getting something outside to letting this imprisoned potential out, freeing you from being dependent on anyone or anything.

ok

"Stage Five: Act As If You're It" once and for all clarifies the commonly misunderstood and misrepresented role of right action in *channeling* this untapped potential rather than *achieving* it, creating a streamlined effect that reduces inner resistance, cutting down the lag time and accelerating the results.

In "Stage Six: Embrace What Appears Broken," you learn a powerful transformational process that gives you the tools to move through those critical thresholds of the mind that unconsciously sabotage your success and turn your flaws and fears into the fertilizer that grows deeper roots and richer fruits, activating the truly extraordinary in you.

"Stage Seven: Wait On the Law" discusses one of the most distinctive features of Emergence: the majority of the work is done below the surface, out of sight. Just as a farmer must nurture a seed and cultivate the soil until it firmly takes root, you must stay committed to what you've planted, instead of jumping from seed to seed seeking short-term gain, or your seeds will never bear fruit. The practice of this principle develops what *A Course In Miracles* calls "the infinite patience [that] produces immediate effects," and is the first step on the path to mastery.[6]

The journey culminates with "Living on the Emerging Edge," where you are invited to become a visionary leader, an instrument for an idea bigger than you—that your life and contribution may help usher in the next stage of human evolution. *let's go*

How to Work with This Book

Books are great tools. But there is always the danger of becoming book smart without gaining true wisdom. The words on the page can lift your consciousness to begin glimpsing your greater potential and seeing what's possible, but only by actively engaging the material and creating a daily practice will you experience real transformation and the gifts of greater aliveness, abundance, and fulfillment. *Action*

This book is structured with each chapter building upon the previous one, so at first it might be best to read it from start to finish and grasp the overall concepts and principles. Once you have a handle on the basics, feel free to dive into any area that inspires you and do—or redo—the work. One suggestion, however, is to take your time. As you read each chapter, be aware of ideas or sentences that cause you to stop and think. That is a hint from your intuition that there's something more there, something between the lines, behind the words. Become still, tune in to that part of you that already has all the answers, and open up to the deeper wisdom that is trying to emerge. In this way, you may not read the book as quickly as you're used to, but when you're done, you won't be the same person who began this journey. *Amen*

And finally, that is what this is: a journey, not a destination. When you realize that there really is no time or space—that everything is happening here and now—you see that there is no place to get to and no final goal to achieve. There is only the continuous discovery and expression of your infinite potential in this moment. That's the only raw material you have to work with; that's all you'll ever have to deal with—this moment. And, as I hope you'll discover through this process, that's more than enough.

Bless you!

FOUNDATION

THE LAW OF EMERGENCE

> More tears are shed over answered prayers
> than unanswered ones.
>
> MOTHER TERESA

Close your eyes for a moment and picture a one-month-old baby in a yellow onesie with rabbits embroidered on it. The baby is sleeping, perhaps cradled softly to someone's chest. Hold that image in your mind and notice what you're thinking about it. How do you feel toward this child?

Are you thinking, "She's so weak, so incapable, and really needs to lose a couple inches around the thighs"? Or, "His hair is thinning, he doesn't even have any teeth yet, all he does is eat and sleep. When is he going to makes something of himself? He's such a burden"?

Sounds ridiculous, huh?

Yet that's how we view ourselves as we grow up and become hypnotized by the cultural beliefs about what constitutes worth, value, and success. We begin to compare ourselves (and others) to everyone else until we have all but lost this awareness of our inherent innocence and perfection.

But there's a place within you that has never stopped seeing yourself through the eyes of love, just as parents see their newborn children. This is the divine within, the presence that eternally holds

income

you in its arms and knows the truth of your perfection. Reconnecting to this original truth is the foundation of Emergence. Without this innate perfection as our starting premise, nothing we do will ever bring us the freedom and fulfillment we seek but will put us on a never-ending treadmill trying to fix, change, or improve what we think is wrong or lacking in order to finally be "enough."

Bonnie, a client of mine, understood this never-ending struggle. A little dynamo, Bonnie was always in motion—a do-gooder, a go-getter, and a caretaker all at once. Don't get me wrong; she's a great person, but a lot of her drive was motivated by the belief that she wasn't enough and that if she could just be more or do more, she would finally become a successful version of herself.

"I just need to figure out how to get this business going," Bonnie said to me in one of our initial phone sessions. "I'm about to lose my house, and if I do, I don't know where on earth my kids and I will go. I've tried so many things, I've spent so much money—money I didn't have—and my life still isn't working out. I don't know why I get myself into these messes. What am I missing that everyone else seems to understand?"

She was near tears as she spoke. I could hear the history in her voice; the subtext was thick, every word weighted down by a story of struggle. Before she finished her sentence, I knew where it was going. I've worked with many people in this situation, and the request is always some version of the same thing: *Can you help me figure out how to bring more money in?* But I'll let you in on a little secret: money is rarely, if ever, the issue, even when it is.

"My life doesn't work" was the real issue. Which was a euphemism for "I don't work. I'm broken. Something is wrong with *me*. And I'm afraid it's not fixable, that I'm not good enough or worthy enough to get what I really want and need." Bonnie is a strong woman with a gentle soul who had been beaten down by circumstances. It's a place we can all recognize, a place we've all lived—many of us still keep a change of clothes there. She just wanted to get out from under the pain, to get a little ahead of the game, to have some assurance that her children would be okay, and, for the love of God, to finally be able to sleep through a single night.

"First, I'm really sorry you're going through this," I said. "It sounds like you've been working *really* hard. You're obviously a good mother."

She held her breath. Then her breathing became shallow, more labored. After thousands of hours listening to clients on the phone, I've developed an ability to read not only the story in their voice but also the meaning in their breathing. Words are powerful clues, but the spaces between the words are often even more potent. It was obvious that she didn't think that highly of herself. But it was deeper than that. I could sense the guilt and shame she carried. She felt like a failure as a mother. Her whole life's struggle was depicted in those few moments of breathing, the staccato bursts of panic followed by the anxious attempt to catch a breath that seemed always to elude her. She had no idea just how deep her struggle was; she was lost in it.

As much as I've been trained to make space for people, my heart breaks a little every time I feel their suffering and I'm unable to fix it for them on the spot. I just want to end it. I wanted to reach through the phone and give her a well-deserved hug. I wanted to give her back to herself. But we can't do that for someone else. We must each reach for ourselves.

Sometimes my work is to comfort the afflicted, but often it is to afflict the comfortable—to shake up the familiar, albeit limited, patterns.

Bonnie wasn't going to like what I had to say.

"The problem is, no matter what you try, as long as you're coming from a place of fear and a feeling that you don't already have what you need, nothing you do will ever get you what you want." I let that sink in, expecting a mini rebellion. Instead, I got silence. I think she was waiting for the punch line. I continued, "What's worse, all your efforts to improve things will just burn you out. Aren't you exhausted by all these attempts to make something happen in your life?"

"Oh, God. You have no idea."

"Believe me, I do. I nearly killed myself twice trying to improve myself!"

That got a laugh. The ice was broken. She breathed a sigh.

"The thing is," I continued, "the life you've been trying to make happen is already happening inside you, but it needs you to be conscious of it and congruent with it. You don't get what you want in life; you get who you *are* in consciousness. Like Gandhi said, you must *become* the change you want to see in the world. Of course, in truth you already are the change you want to see; you just need to *know* it."

"I've done so much work on myself!" She was exasperated, at her wit's end, and the last thing she wanted from me was a lecture. "Clearly I'm doing something wrong." She lapsed back into beating herself up; she had become a pro at that. Many of us have. That's what happens when we believe that we're not good enough and that we need something or someone else to make us better.

"You didn't do it wrong. You did what you've been taught. *It's not your fault.*" Those words can be a lifeline. Grab hold of them and they can stop a downward spiral. "The problem is you're stuck on this idea of what you think your life should look like and how you think things should work out, but the truth is, you have no idea how things should work out."

That got another laugh. "You've got that right!"

"But there is something inside you that *does*. A perfect pattern and a divine intelligence that knows how to bring it into expression."

"So will this bring some money in?"

"No." I paused. A pause is a wonderful thing. It allows things to sink in or things to rise up. "This source within you doesn't bring more into your life; it pulls more life out of *you*. The result is what appears to be more things coming *to* you but is really more of *you* emerging."

"So will *that* get my business working?" She seemed embarrassed to ask again.

"I don't know." I paused again. I knew she wanted to hear a definite yes, and in my heart I wanted to give it to her. But I also knew she'd been given the "right answer" by many people before, trying to placate her fears or sell her the next get-rich-quick program. She needed to dig deeper if she was going to experience lasting change.

"What *do* you know?" She was frustrated again but also apologetic. She wasn't the type to express anger (something she *needed* to access her power, which I later helped her do and will talk about in Stage Six).

"What I know is that when you make the connection to this seed of potential within you and become aligned with it, *whatever* you need for your life to emerge to the next level will show up. If that's your business, that's what you'll get."

"So, how do I do that?"

The Missing Link

Like the thousands of people I've worked with over the years, Bonnie had looked to many modalities for self-improvement, manifestation, and success in order to bring things into her life she believed she was lacking. For her, she attached it all to having a successful business or, more accurately, money. She didn't really care about the business; it was a means to an end.

For others, it's a new mate, a promotion, a car, a house, or a healing. And in some cases it works initially. Even Bonnie had some early success with these other approaches (getting a "great deal" on the house she was now on the verge of losing).

The problem was that she manifested the bigger home but didn't develop "bigger home consciousness." Meaning, she changed the world outside but remained the same inside. She was bumping up against a primary problem with many personal development strategies: When they're not applied in the larger context of Emergence—in the realization that everything is already within us—they often become just metaphysical versions of physical actions. In other words, instead of struggling physically to manipulate circumstances, the individual struggles mentally and emotionally to achieve the same results.

It might be a step up from manual labor—there's definitely more leverage when we use our mind over matter—but there's rarely much transformational value in it. And because it's still based on a sense of being separate and needing something you don't already have, it can feel just as exhausting as trying to chop down a tree with a hand ax. Even some sincere spiritual teachings, still rooted in a dualistic perception of life, teach followers to use this great power within to get more stuff out there, which often leads to spiritual materialism (where we use the spirit to attain more materially, instead of using our material experience to grow spiritually) and perpetuates the very problems they're trying to heal.

When you practice any goal-achieving technique that starts from a premise that you're broken or lacking or something is missing, your growth is determined by the level of your current self-image—the picture you have of yourself that is made up of your perceptions, fears, and past traumas as well as the stories you tell yourself and the characters you play in those stories. At best, this creates superficial improvements.

What we create will always be *congruent with* our current self-image, so any improvement we attempt will still carry the underlying fears and limited beliefs we have about ourselves, which can only lead to the same stress and struggle. At worst, these efforts can actually magnify our underlying issues and create even bigger problems down the road.

In contrast, when we recognize that everything we need is already within us and begin to reconnect to that feeling of innate wholeness and perfection—the way we felt toward that baby—we lay the foundation for the Law of Emergence to operate a process that is about becoming (or, rather, revealing) more of who you truly are, unleashing your infinite, often imprisoned potential. On this path, there is never a danger of going the wrong way or hitting a dead end because rather than trying to fix, correct, or fill in something that is missing, the Law of Emergence holds that when you cultivate your inner conditions, your next evolutionary stage will unfold organically. And because your next stage is already within you, it will arrive *whole*, bringing with it everything needed for its fulfillment.

This isn't to say you should do away with all your success strategies or personal development tools. As larger paradigms arc discovered, previous ideas are often folded into them. After all, we didn't do away with the wheel when our preferred mode of transportation evolved from the horse and buggy to the automobile. We still use wheels, only now instead of being pulled by something outside our vehicle, the car is powered by the engine under the hood. Likewise, the Law of Emergence contains the principles of planning, action, attraction, self-awareness, spiritual connection, and all the other elements necessary to creating the life you deeply desire. But as you activate your Emergence, you won't have to work these other laws. As you realize you're already who you're meant to be and you already have the thing you want, your process will become more about Self-realization. As a byproduct, the universal laws will continue to operate to draw to you—or, more accurately, *from you*—everything you need to achieve your true potential.

It's also important to understand that Self-realization is not a straight line. It's like the oak with its far-reaching root system and outstretched branches as it grows from sapling to mature tree. We're all at different developmental stages in various areas of our life, and you might still need to work with other practices to stabilize your human structures (those core areas that make up a complete person, such as health, wealth, relationships, work, and spirituality). Just as a tree does, we may need additional support to hold it upright while it grows through certain stages.

So if you're struggling to meet your basic monetary needs, you may need to learn more about wealth, abundance, and fiscal responsibility until that area is strong enough that it doesn't siphon off your energy. If you're battling to maintain basic health, you may need a gym membership, a trainer, or a new diet so that your physical issues don't take you out of the game. If you're dealing with deep-seated trauma, seeing a therapist is not a bad idea.

Every stage of our development serves a purpose in getting us to the next level. Babies crawl before they walk, cry before they talk, and play with blocks before constructing a building. We're always in the act of Emergence, and if we don't interfere with the process, we'll keep evolving to the next stage. The key is to not become attached to or overly identified with any practice or condition. Just keep ascending higher. Because the Law of Emergence is about tapping into the Self that is already whole, complete, and infinite in scope, practicing its principles while you're strengthening any of the areas mentioned here will ensure that you remain on the emerging edge no matter what conditions you find yourself in. For now, just consider that many of the ways you've learned to manifest, attract, or create your life are part of an old evolutionary paradigm, and be prepared for a quantum leap up the evolutionary ladder—a growth spurt, if you will.

The main purpose of this chapter (and book) is to give you a deeper knowledge of the core psychological and spiritual principles and practices that make up and support the Law of Emergence to help you navigate your own Emergence with an understanding of what's happening inside, a solid grasp on how it works, and the confidence to know it's working. Emergence works whether or not you know how or why, but having this foundation tends to make it work better, faster, and more consistently. There may be times when you become confused or frustrated with the ideas being presented. Take heart. This is not only normal; it's necessary. It means that a new, higher idea is trying to emerge through old conditioned thinking. I invite you to use this as an opportunity to dig your roots deeper through journaling and further contemplation. This often results in breakthrough insights, life-changing paradigm shifts, and new ways of seeing and being in the world.

In any case, don't let yourself become bogged down by the paralysis of overanalysis. Let the seeds of these ideas fall upon the fertile soil of your soul, water them with your willingness to grow, and keep plowing forward. This is a path of revelation; you will be revealed to yourself. I can tell you from my own journey and from my experiences of being a guide for many others that there's nothing more amazing and fulfilling than discovering who you really are and the world of possibility waiting for you. It's also a path of revolution; it will help you overthrow the old entrenched ways of being that have oppressed your potential and will liberate you in ways beyond your imagination.

So what happened to Bonnie? Well, as she began to walk her own path of Emergence, she discovered who she really was, who she had always been but had forgotten. The thing she thought she needed—improving her business—did not happen. Instead, she got a job that paid the bills, which gave her enough relief to get back in touch with one of her true loves: music. This led to her joining a band, where she fell in love with one of the members and embarked on a whole new adventure of romance, passion, and possibility that she hadn't dreamed of before.

The Acorn Principle

Because many of us hold a belief that our fate is determined by external conditions and that the things we need are "out there"—the reverse of how life really works—we constantly struggle against the natural order of the universe.

The basic false belief goes something like this:

We are born blank slates, empty shells, and must make something of ourselves—internally and externally. The knowledge, resources, and support systems we need to achieve this are outside us, in other people, other places—or higher powers—that are hard to get to, requiring us to conform to cultural, societal, or religious norms to get them, often demanding that we work really hard at something we don't love for most of our life and engage in a religious practice that gives us more guilt than good, all so we can save enough money to start living our life and accrue enough karmic credits to survive our afterlife, only to die before we get to really live.

Whether or not you consciously buy into that B.S. (belief system), you're probably living it to some degree because it's part of the collective consciousness of much of the Westernized world and is rapidly being adopted by developing countries in an effort to achieve social stability and economic freedom. Meeting our expanding needs is a necessary and even noble goal, but if the underlying beliefs and value systems guiding it *are in opposition to the fundamental harmony of the universe*, it will ultimately result in more suffering and limitation.

So what does the acorn principle have to do with this? For one, it reveals how to harness the power of the universe rather than oppose it. By understanding this aspect of Mother Nature, you will discover a vital clue to your own nature and how you were designed to grow. As we've touched upon, the acorn already contains the perfect pattern and potential to become an oak. It's not an empty shell that has to struggle, figure out how life works, gather a bunch of information to fill itself with, and finally decide what it wants to be when it grows up. No matter the opinion of other trees in the forest, the acorn will never become anything but what's inside it—an oak. Even if its parent oak wants it to grow up to be an apple tree, it's not going to happen. It might fail to thrive or reach its potential if the right conditions aren't created, but *the acorn's destiny is to become an oak.* The big questions of life, such as "Who am I?" and "What is my purpose?" were answered before the seed was planted in the ground.

The Principle of Correspondence, a Hermetic law, states, "As above so below; as within so without."[1] This means that whatever happens on one level of reality also happens on every other level, or the microcosm and the macrocosm. Therefore, by understanding the deeper nature of something you can observe, you can infer the nature of a parallel something you *can't* observe as easily. In other words, there is really only one ultimate reality—it's just being perceived from different levels and angles. Michael Coleman Talbot described this point of view as the "Holographic Universe" principle.[2] The identification of this principle, along with other correlations in interdisciplinary studies, led some scientists and philosophers, such as Ralph Waldo Emerson and Albert Einstein, to the conclusion that the same processes that occur in nature—and their underlying principles—can be found in other areas of life.

For many natural laws, there is often a parallel moral, scientific, and spiritual law that mirrors it. For example, the positive and negative charge required to conduct an electric current can be correlated to the masculine and feminine energy that must come together to create new life; the masculine and feminine is correlated to the left and right hemispheres of the brain and its functions; and the concept of yin and yang in Chinese philosophy, medicine, and science reflects a multitude of contradictory yet interdependent dualities found in nature—fire and water, light and dark, the sun and the moon.

To put it poetically, William Blake wrote in "Auguries of Innocence," "To see a world in a grain of sand, and a heaven in a wild
flower, hold infinity in the palm of your hand, and eternity in an
hour."[3] Einstein, who coined the term "unified field theory" (also
called the "theory of everything") in an attempt to create a theory
that included and explained all the major principles of physics,
believed that if we could fully comprehend the laws of the universe,
we could know the mind of God.[4]

From this fundamental idea of balance and unity that persists
wherever we look closely enough, we could reason that the basic
laws governing the acorn—or any seed—apply to the seed of our
own being, which already contains the blueprint and mechanics for
its perfect materialization. Just as the oak is already in the acorn
before the acorn is planted in the ground, everything you need to
fulfill your destiny was already in you before you were planted in
your mother's womb.

In his book *The Soul's Code,*[5] James Hillman discusses the idea
of the acorn as a metaphor for how our destiny unfolds, although the
concept of a destiny, calling, or "governing image" in our soul has
been articulated throughout the ages—in the Kabbalah, Buddhism,
Hinduism, Plato's *Republic*, and many indigenous cultures. In the
context of Emergence, however, the acorn analogy is taken to the next
level: Locked up in the seed of your soul is not just an image, calling, or pattern of potential; it is the fully realized Self, formed in the
invisible dimension of your being. And while it makes use of the raw
materials of your life to take shape, it is not dependent on anything
outside of you for its existence, as it already possesses the power and
substance to manifest whatever it needs

As Hillman pointed out, you can see signs of this pattern of
potential in children who, without any external conditioning—or
despite it—become interested in things that don't reflect their parents,' siblings,' or cultural influences. There's something unique

unfolding that seems to come from within them. Why do two children growing up in the same home with largely the same experiences go on to pursue such different professions as a priest and a plumber or a cop and a crook? Can the nurture argument really explain that? Can it explain a da Vinci, whose parents had nothing to do with the arts, or a Mozart, who became a master pianist and violinist at age four and created his first symphony at age five?

Hillman even suggests—and I agree—that many seemingly aberrant behaviors of children (and some adults) are actually evidence of inner conflict between the seed of their calling and their undeveloped conscious mind. On some level, these children sense this great destiny within them but don't have the psychological or emotional facility to deal with it, which results in what we call behavioral issues. Traditional psychology often attempts to "heal" children of these perceived behavioral problems instead of working to recognize them as possible expressions of a child's inner destiny, and, in turn, an underdeveloped psyche trying to comprehend these expressions. However sincere the intentions of doctors, teachers, and parents may be, we must ask ourselves: How many geniuses have been suppressed because what was trying to emerge was not understood? How many masterpieces, inventions, and innovations are we repressing with our societal pressure to conform to certain norms of being good boys and girls?

Maybe while growing up you had tendencies that were misunderstood and were wrongly judged as being problematic or "weird." Because of this, you may have developed guilt or shame around your unique thoughts, feelings, and actions. Maybe you even repressed them out of fear or confusion or a desire to fit in, be loved and accepted, or not rock the boat.

As a kid, I had a strong desire to create, whether pinging out the boogie-woogie on our baby grand, shooting sci-fi movies on my Sears Super 8 reflex camera, or lying under my covers with a flashlight, filling a sketchpad with utopian worlds. One might have described me as a hyperactive child (which they did) or a dreamer with my head in the clouds (which they did) and attributed no other significance to those activities (which they didn't). In my teens, I developed a strong desire to learn about my friends' religions: Christianity, Judaism, Buddhism—you name it, I was fascinated by it. I also had a strong urge to see and affirm the good in people, which one friend referred to as the "love bomb" because I would spontaneously compliment him for no reason. My friends thought I was weird, and I didn't entirely disagree. After all, it wasn't the typical behavior of any "normal" teenagers I knew. I didn't understand where all this was coming from or where it was going. It was just who I was.

As I learned to honor these impulses, even when I didn't understand them, and to cultivate conditions that supported them, the seeds that had once seemed so strange grew into the strong trunk and deep roots of a rewarding and varied life. Likewise, you have a unique chance to revisit the aspects of your character that have been present since childhood and discover who you really are. The signs of your true Self have been there from the beginning. Look at the things you were or still are interested in—the activities that made you lose track of time, your daydreams, your favorite movies, reading materials, or people you admired or idolized—and you'll see numerous clues pointing to your purpose. We'll go deeper into this in "Stage One: See the Completed Vision."

The truth—as the great spiritual masters have taught—is that all of life is conspiring for our awakening and fulfillment. Just as there are certain plants that *require* rough soil to activate chemicals that make them heartier and better able to thrive in their environment, the challenges I faced created the perfect conditions for my growth, compelling me to push my roots deeper and strengthen my inner structures. Like certain seeds that need a forest fire to germinate, those early childhood experiences sparked a fire within me that cracked open the seed of my potential and allowed it to grow. What I can now see is that all these powerful promptings were my acorn (or true Self) guiding and directing me, creating opportunities for me to cultivate the inner and outer conditions necessary for its emergence. The same process is true for you.

Indigenous vs. Endogenous

If, like an acorn, you needed the right conditions to grow, we would be back to the problem of existing at the whim of external forces. But here's where human nature has been given a capacity beyond Mother Nature. Whereas the acorn is indigenous (originating or occurring naturally in a particular place) and therefore can only thrive in certain external conditions not within its control, human beings are endogenous (having an internal cause of origin), which means that your conditions are internally derived or generated. It doesn't matter what external conditions you're planted in. *Your soul is your soil*, and if you generate the right *inner conditions*—mentally, emotionally, and spiritually—your seed will have the right nutrients to thrive. What's more, whereas most seeds require external light to grow, human beings are self-effulgent, meaning we generate light from within. This is not only a spiritual fact discernable through meditation; scientists have detected that human beings actually "glimmer" with measurable light via photon emission.[6] No matter how thick the clouds may be outside or how dark the night, the light is always shining within, ready to illuminate the seed of your true Self and nourish its growth.

Genesis 1:27 says, "God created man in His own image." This principle is stated in different ways by most religions, and it's sometimes interpreted to mean that we have the same physical features as God. It's like the metaphysical joke: God made man in His own image, and man has been trying to return the favor ever since! In other words, we keep trying to understand God in human, material terms, like some anthropomorphic being sitting on a cloud. But this is an overly literal interpretation of ancient teachings. In John 4:24, it is said that "God is *spirit*, and those who worship Him must worship in spirit and truth." Or, from the Tao Te Ching, "The Tao that can be told is not the eternal Tao; the name that can be named is not the eternal Name." Mystically understood, being "created in His own image" doesn't mean we "look" like God; it means we possess the same constituent qualities, which have been described as spirit, truth, love, beauty, power, and intelligence, among others, just as the wave contains the same elements as the ocean. Psalms 82:6 says, "You are gods, children of the Most High." Essentially, we're just chips off the Old Block.

This divine inheritance includes our ability to decide what we focus our awareness on (i.e., free will) and the creative power of our consciousness. And because our focus determines what's in our consciousness and our consciousness determines our experience, we ultimately have a godlike power over our world. As William Ernest Henley wrote in his powerful poem "Invictus," you are "the master of [your] fate, the captain of [your] soul."[7] No matter what side of the tracks you were born on, what kind of childhood you had, what current challenges you're slogging through, or what race, color, orientation, creed, or age you are, when you create the right *inner conditions*, the great purpose for which you were born *must* emerge.

The Self vs. the self

We have been born under a case of mistaken identity. Almost everything we see, hear, and experience—almost everything produced by society—keeps us in the dark about who and what we truly are. Our mistaken identity is that we are merely human beings having an occasional spiritual experience; that we are born in sin, circumscribed by our personality, a product of our culture and family, conceived on a certain date, destined to die. But our true nature is exactly the opposite. Philosopher Pierre Teilhard de Chardin expressed the truth when he said, "We are not human beings having a spiritual experience. We are spiritual beings having a human experience."[8]

When we peel away the dogma and doctrine of all great spiritual teachings, we discover that they have been trying to wake us up from the illusion, or *maya*, as it's called in some schools of Hinduism. Sin, as it turns out, is not some demonic quality of our soul; the word is an archery term that means to miss the mark. The only original sin we were born with is this false belief about who we are.

The fact that this human self we perceive isn't who we really are doesn't mean it's bad or that we should subjugate it (as some extreme religious practices have concluded). This human incarnation is a magnificent thing, like a work of art, with the potential to reveal great beauty and meaning. But it's a pale reflection of the truth, just as looking at a painting of your beloved pales in comparison to being with them. Your true Self is, as Genesis 1:27 puts it, "made in the image and likeness of God"—eternal, changeless, and infinite—whereas your human self is made in the image and likeness of your history and culture and the many changes that arise out of the Self and dissolve back into it. Everything you need for your total fulfillment is already within you, constituted as a part of this essential Self. And when you are more identified with your true Self and learn to depend on it for everything, all your needs will emerge without the effort and struggle so common to the human experience.

I remember the first time this principle became real for me. It was before I stood on that stage mentioned in the beginning of this book and before I had the words to explain it. It was an initiation, something we all have at a certain point—often many points—on the path of personal growth. Such an experience forces us to move beyond mere intellectual understanding or belief and *prove* the truth of the principles we're trying to live by, transforming our theoretical knowledge into working wisdom.

I had quit acting, stopped watching television and reading newspapers, and pretty much cloistered myself in my small North Hollywood apartment (decorated like some bad '70s show, with a pea-green fridge and Formica counters), meditating, praying, and journaling about the inner journey I was making. At a certain point, I had gone through my savings, had no work or future prospects, and had exhausted all external means of support. I was left with nothing but my spiritual insights—literally living on a prayer. I was also, to be honest, pretty pissed off at God. I mean, there I was, dedicating my life to spiritual practice, trying to be a light in the world, and I couldn't even pay my light bill!

One day, after groveling for another rent extension from my landlord, I sat in my worn faux-leather meditation chair and laid down the gauntlet: *God, either there really is a true Self with everything it needs to fulfill its purpose or this is all a bunch of bull. Either way, I'm gonna find out today, because I'm not getting up until I have my answer.* I like to think of this as my Gary Sinise moment from *Forrest Gump*, where Lieutenant Dan is on top of the ship's mast in the raging storm, railing against the Almighty, basically saying, "Bring it on!" So there I sat, and sat, as daylight turned into dark and the choir of crickets began their nightly chorus. I meditated and prayed and beseeched and surrendered, trying to reconnect to this essential Self I had touched in my brush-with-death experience in that coral reef. Wave after wave of emotion rolled through me, threatening to drown me again, with no end in sight.

Then at some point in the middle of the night, after wrestling with my demons and feeling pinned to the mat, it was as if a voice spoke to me and said, "You made your savings account your source, your god, and whenever you make something outside of you the source of your security or supply, the universe is set up to betray you—so that you'll turn within and find your real Source again." I half expected Moses to be standing there, looking a lot like Charlton Heston, waving one of his tablets: "Thou shalt have no other gods before me!" That commandment suddenly thundered with a new mystical meaning. And in that moment, it was like a pressure valve opened inside my body, draining me of all anxiety. A peace washed over me, a peace that "passeth all understanding," as Philippians 4:7 puts it. I crawled into bed and fell asleep.

For the next few days, I went about my business, actually forgetting that I had a problem. When I remembered, "Oh, yeah, I have all these bills due and not a damn clue how to pay them," there wasn't the usual fear or frustration gripping me but instead an inner feeling that things would be okay, like I was now being held by something bigger than my personal capacity to manage things.

And then the phone rang.

It was my former acting agent, calling me with an audition. He said he knew I was "too spiritual" to do commercials anymore (I was, let's just say, a little "out there" back then), but a casting director had called out of the blue, requesting me. I immediately knew it was my answer and accepted the audition. I booked the commercial, and in two days I earned enough money to pay for a year's worth of living expenses.

There are a few key elements to this experience that I want to highlight. First, I didn't have any plan. I didn't create a vision board or visualize a particular desired outcome. I just reconnected to that part of me that was *already whole*, had a *feeling* of my innate completeness, and then surrendered my control of the outcome. By making this connection, I cultivated the conditions in consciousness that allowed it to naturally emerge. Had I tried to visualize the outcome, I might have fantasized a variety of things, from getting a job as a spiritual teacher or writer (which I was unqualified for), to winning the lottery or receiving an inheritance from a long-lost uncle (one can always dream). But I never would have imagined my ex-agent calling me and booking a commercial because that idea *was outside of my known self* as a "spiritual guy" who didn't act anymore.

I'm not saying you shouldn't create a plan or use visualization and affirmations. Those tools have a place in cultivating the conscious conditions for your Emergence. But in order to allow your greatest good to express itself in the most powerful way, you must identify less as a limited human self that is trapped in time and instead tune in to the boundless eternal Self within. At first, as in my case, doing so might help you pay your rent and put food on the table. Meeting your basic survival needs is often one of the initial results of making this connection. But the underlying principle has more profound implications. The realization of your essential Self and the resulting activation of the Law of Emergence can transform every aspect of your life—and those lives that touch yours—ending conflict, dissolving fear, and creating a world that works for the highest good of everyone. Once we *know* we're already whole and that everything we need is within us—including love, respect, validation, power, wealth, and health—we realize there's no reason to demand, fight for, or fear the loss of any of this.

We spin our wheels trying to come up with solutions to all our social, political, personal, and professional problems. We create new policies, more restrictive laws, bigger prisons, and more powerful weapons to attack the issues or just twist ourselves into knots trying to solve things. But no matter what new invention or theory we come up with or what practice we engage in, if it doesn't arise out of our true Self-realization—out of an awareness of our innate wholeness—it will never create lasting peace, abundance, or fulfillment in our lives or on the planet.

Besides these broader implications, an understanding of our true Self versus our human self is a primary condition in the successful activation of the Law of Emergence. To the extent that you identify with the part of you that is changing—the human self—you create resistance to the part of you that is emerging—the true Self—much the way an acorn would if it identified with its shell instead of the oak. What's more, to the extent that you identify with the Self that changes, the Self that appears lacking, you come under the human laws of limitation and perpetuate them in your experience. This prevents our evolution. We keep trying to solve the problems created by the human mind and its limited or distorted perceptions—problems such as separation, self-preservation, competition, and conflict—using the same mind-set that created them. But you can never solve a problem from the same level of consciousness that created it.

When, however, you identify more with your changeless, boundless Self, you stay rooted in your core, even as your human incarnation and external world continue to change form and reveal your ever-expanding good. You no longer live from the level the problems were created on. You stop doing the same thing over and over, expecting different results. You enter into a peace and fulfillment no longer dependent on external conditions but supported and fueled by the whole universe.

From Cause and Effect to Grace

Many of the world's religions, when interpreted from a more literal perspective, sometimes teach that we're at the whim of an external God who rewards or punishes us for good and bad deeds, like Santa with his naughty-or-nice list, or who just acts in capricious, mysterious ways we're not intended to understand. But a more spiritual or mystical interpretation of the Christian teaching "as you sow so shall you reap," the Buddhist teaching of karma, or the metaphysical law of attraction suggests that there is no external power. It is the seeds we sow in our own heart and mind—the overall quality of our consciousness—that cause us to reap the rewards and punishment we experience.

While this is a liberating truth and a great step up the evolutionary ladder, it can also be an overwhelming realization. If all the things we've thought, said, and done in the past (or past lifetimes) are creating our present and, ultimately, our future, won't it take the rest of our lives (or many more lifetimes) to undo the mess we've created? A lot of causes have been set in motion. How will we ever reverse all their effects?

Mercifully, there is a higher law: Grace. The Law of Grace says that no matter what has come before, no matter what you've set in motion, when you reconnect with the truth of your being—this perfect seed pattern the world has never touched and can never destroy—the innate wholeness, wisdom, and power you need will emerge again. From this consciousness, your past does not determine your future. Neither do past mistakes nor past lives. The bad seeds you've sown are uprooted no matter how deeply they've dug in, and the good seeds you've failed to tend take root and bear fruit. Under the Law of Grace, the things you're struggling with lose their power. Cause and effect, karma, even Newtonian physics, which once operated as absolute, immutable laws and masters of your fate, become the servants of your destiny.

The relative nature of cause and effect has been investigated through subjects such as quantum entanglement, a phenomenon where two or more objects once linked together remain connected and responsive to each other even when they're separated by vast expanses in space, and nonlocal healing, which has explored through randomized double-blind studies the power of prayer to heal patients at a distance.[9]

These and other discoveries are beginning to reveal how rather than living in a linear material world that reacts in a logical cause-and-effect fashion (as provided in Newton's third law of motion, which says that for every action there is an equal and opposite reaction), we exist in an indivisible unified field, out of which all creation arises. On the surface, things appear separate and solid—and at that relative level there appears to be cause and effect—but as we dive deeper, we discover that the "solid" world is in fact completely made up of invisible energy and information. The atom, once believed to be the building block of all material reality, is in fact 99.9 percent empty space.

At this deeper level, reality doesn't operate the way it does at the grosser material level. Things are not linear or bound by space and time. This underlying intelligence seems to be simultaneously everywhere (omnipresent), with a knowledge of everything (omniscient), and is the only power there is (omnipotent). In short, it could be described as an *omni-active intelligence with infinite organizing power in a field of unbounded potentiality*. That also happens to be how many mystics, prophets, and, to some extent, religions have described God and how many cutting-edge scientists are describing consciousness. Rather than there being interactivity among all things—the basis of cause and effect—there is an omni-activity. One action. At the deepest level, something is emerging—an infinite idea unfolding—and as it breaks into time and space, it appears as if certain things are interacting and in turn causing other things to happen, but that's a trick of the senses.

Here we arrive back at our central idea: inside the seed of you—indeed, the seed of the whole world—there is a design for its fulfillment. Things are not unfolding by chance. You are not at the mercy of other causes. Things are not happening *to* you; they are happening *through* you. There is an underlying order or pattern that is already perfect and seeking to emerge from within your soul, just waiting for the right conditions. And everything is conspiring to create those conditions, regardless of what you've been through or where you currently are. As Ralph Waldo Emerson said, "The dice of God are always loaded."[10] The entire universe is rigged in your favor.

And this is where Grace comes in.

Grace is the realization that no matter what appears on the surface of life, no matter what has come before or what appears to be lost, when you tap back into this perfect seed pattern, it will emerge again, fresh, vital, overflowing with new possibilities. Whereas the rules of karma say you're destined to live out the effects of your previous causes, the realization of Grace is that in a "Holy Instant,"[11] your life can be made new and "though your sins are as scarlet, they will be as white as snow" (Isaiah 1:18).

Furthermore, whereas traditional thinking often dictates that the effects you experience are limited by the causes you can personally set in motion at a human level—usually determined by external conditions seemingly beyond your control—when you align with the perfect pattern seeking to emerge from within, it will not only move you personally into right action but also move your entire world if necessary to reveal your greater purpose. As my example about paying the rent demonstrated, my seeming lack of human solutions didn't matter. The moment I connected with this higher Self, it moved people and events beyond the limits of my personal sphere of influence and delivered exactly what I needed. A familiar Old Testament passage sums up this all-powerful Emergence of Grace: "Every valley shall be exalted, and every mountain and hill shall be made low; and the uneven shall be made level, and the rough places a plain"(Isaiah 40:4).

As we consider how Grace works, we arrive at an inescapable conclusion: if we can affect this unified field with our consciousness, and this field is omnipresent and indivisible, then we must be it and it must be us. There can be no separate self—no subject/

object relationship—in an omnipresence. Here, the deeper esoteric meaning behind two rarely understood Biblical statements reveals itself—"The Kingdom of Heaven is *within you*"(Luke 17:20-21) and "*You* are the Light of the world" (Matthew 5:14). Or to reference Hindu philosophy, one's true self (Atman) is identical with the transcendent self (Brahman).

In other words, *you* are this infinite omnipresent something that is forever unfolding. Not the human you—who was born, has a history, and will eventually dissolve back into dust—but the real you, the true Self that is always emerging. This is the ultimate truth illuminated by all great religions, spiritual masters, and, in many ways, the laws of the physical world we live in but that has often, even with good intentions, been obscured by an overly literal, materialistic interpretation of these ancient teachings.

With this understanding of your true Self and the power of Grace, you are no longer beholden to external powers or authority; you are no longer a prisoner of past experience or present conditions. Combined with an understanding that you are not a limited physical person but part of the larger fabric of existence—like a wave upon the ocean, never separate—you are now equipped with a bold new picture of how reality works. You can release the struggle of self-improvement, manifestation, and attraction. You can surrender to this deeper sense of harmony and order and begin to consciously activate the Law of Emergence in powerful, life-changing ways.

The
SEVEN STAGES
of
EMERGINEERING

SEE THE COMPLETED VISION

Where there is no vision, the people perish.

PROVERBS 29:18

Picture an acorn on the forest floor.

It's a small, leathery, cuplike shell containing an even smaller seed—a seed that, given the right conditions, will emerge into a mighty oak.

It seems so normal, so natural, that a giant tree would come from a tiny seed. We rarely question the impossible physics of such a feat. Where, for example, in that tiny seed is the "stuff" of an oak stored and the factory to produce it? Where are the blueprints, the brain, the intricate network of intelligence necessary to transform that tiny oak fruit into the mythical oak?

For many, science hasn't yet fully explained how such things happen. Even the theory of evolution seems incomplete when we consider the complexity that emerges from a few particles of carbon material, which are really just stardust.

So where is the oak *before* it emerges through the acorn?

One might argue that there is no "oak" as a singular something, that it's the random result of many smaller somethings. It's just what happens when the principles of life—mathematics, physics, biology—collide.

Are all these laws, principles, and patterns "created" every time an oak emerges from an acorn? If not, where are they, and were they ever created? In other words, was there a time when mathematics didn't exist? Even before we knew what it was, even before there was a "we" here to contemplate it, two plus two still equaled four. People could have built airplanes and computers during the time of Buddha if they had tapped the then still-hidden secrets that made such advancements possible, because all these ideas, patterns, and the capacity to manifest them *have always existed*.

They exist in the same place the oak does before it emerges.

The same is true for you and the vision of your life.

A Vision Is Never in the Future

Within you is a destiny waiting to be born. Not within your body but within the part of you that has always existed. In order to fulfill it, you must tap into your soul's vision.

But what is a vision? How do we create it?

True vision can neither be created nor changed because it's part of this ultimate reality we've been exploring—what Plato called the realm of perfect prototypes or ideal forms. It comes from a place beyond the mind, beyond time, beyond space, and beyond experience. And because of this, a true vision is not a picture of what will be in the future; it's a realization of *what is* in the timeless dimension of your consciousness.

Your tomorrow is an extension of God's today. Think of it like standing above an ant as it travels across the ground toward a potato chip, which the ant can't see because the chip is obscured by a hill. From the ant's point of view, the vision of lunch is in its future, but from yours it's in the present. The ant, the journey, and the potato chip are all here now. The same is true for your vision. From a larger perspective, it's already happening.

What's more, the vision is not static; it's transformational. As you allow it to infuse you with its energy and rhythms, it stretches and reshapes you, accelerating your growth and expansion. As you begin to see that everything you're waiting, working, or hoping for in the future is already here now, within you, it challenges and changes the way you think, feel, and act in virtually every area of your life. You begin to break your dependence on external conditions and rely more on inner ones that you have control over. You move from *getting* things to fill yourself up to *letting* more of your infinite Self out. You stop trying to make it happen and instead *make it welcome* by developing a deeper connection to this inner seed of potential and cultivating the soil of your soul for new growth.

This is the foundation for real vision. Establishing it activates the first stage of the Law of Emergence.

Visualization vs. Vision

Many people who endeavor to live their best life, particularly in the self-help and success arena, turn to a well-known form of creative imagination called visualization, a process of holding in mind the image of some desired outcome until, through the Law of Mind Action (also referred to as the Law of Attraction), you bring it into form. This can be a useful tool for many short-term goals. If you focus on an image long enough, with enough feeling, you can manifest some version of it, whether it's an improved golf swing, a parking space, or a family vacation. But attempts to visualize your larger life often result in manifesting only an improved version of your limited self-concept—a shinier acorn but rarely an oak. What's worse, any time we forcibly manifest something from this limited self-concept, it carries with it the seeds of its own destruction.

I've struggled with this dilemma on my journey, going back and forth between answering the deeper call of vision to becoming impatient and using visualization to manifest what I wanted, only to run into the same problems I'd had before, just at a higher level. Years ago when I was feeling stuck in a certain financial bracket, I worked intensely with many of the traditional tools of manifestation to expand my income and lifestyle, complete with a bigger car, a bigger house, and a bigger monthly budget. My efforts were successful and I felt great—momentarily. Underneath it all, I hadn't realized the true vision for my life; I was just attracting more stuff based on my limited self-image. Soon enough my unresolved issues came out, bringing the same stress and financial worries, just at a higher income level. In fact, it was more stressful because now I had more money, relationships, and responsibilities to deal with. The inner structures hadn't been strengthened and couldn't handle the heavier load. I had changed the superficial picture of my world, but I remained fundamentally the same.

In a state of overwhelm, I decided to slow down and spend more time meditating and journaling again. And as I became still in the midst of this crisis, I discovered a deeper impulse, a more authentic dimension of myself trying to emerge, which I had suppressed, as my fear of lack and sense of inadequacy drove me to artificially manifest what I thought I needed to be secure and worthy. It took a degree of faith and a willingness to let my life fall apart in order for it to fall together at a higher level. This didn't mean that my life *had* to fall apart, just that I had to be *willing* to let it; I had to let go of attachment, of my ideas of what should or shouldn't be. And in that space of surrender, and with a healthy dose of humility, I was finally able to answer the call of a deeper vision. I became more aligned with my authentic self—bringing with it not only greater abundance but also a greater sense of ease and purpose.

Many of my clients have come to me after visualizing themselves into new relationships, better-looking bodies, bigger houses, or more money (all of which could have been looked at as successful manifestations), only to discover that their real purpose wasn't being fulfilled by these outer trappings, leaving them more exhausted and disillusioned. They'd gotten what they wanted but not what they truly needed. Each time they were willing to surrender to the deeper vision within them, however, and do the work of becoming congruent with it (which we'll get to in Stage Two), their life was taken to a new level.

The pressure we feel to keep up with the Joneses and the complex facades we build to support this imitation of success become so much a part of our identity, it can feel like our whole world would have to collapse in order for it to get back on track. But that doesn't have to be your story. While it's true that we must let go of the old, sometimes cherished parts of our inner and outer life to let the new emerge—just as the acorn must release the protective shell to become an oak and the caterpillar must release its familiar form to grow wings—when we tap into the greater vision of our life and live from that deeper place, the joy, inspiration, and adventure of Emergence far outweigh the temporary birth pains.

Visualization and other manifestation techniques (vision boards, affirmations, and so on) are useful tools, but they aren't enough. With them alone you can only fulfill your ego's desire, not your soul's destiny, nor, for that matter, the highest purpose of a project, relationship, or business. This approach keeps you stuck in a cycle of visualization-manifestation-visualization-manifestation, round and round, never finding peace or satisfaction. In order to go beyond that, you must move from visualization to vision, from mind-projected images based on limited self-concepts to the divine ideas planted in your soul.

From Imagination to Emergination

Imagination is often hailed as one of the greatest tools of innovation. Even Einstein said, "Imagination is more important than knowledge."[1] And I would agree. Imagination is a powerful faculty that allows us to take charge of our thoughts and gain some control over our experience. Mastering this faculty helps us realize that our environment doesn't determine our destiny and permits us to move from passive victim to active creator.

But imagination, as we often understand and use it, is limited by our experience, self-concepts, or the collective beliefs of our culture. Therefore, it can only build on what's already known; it's just a new twist on the content already in our consciousness. It's like rearranging the furniture in a room that's too small for your purposes or built on a foundation that can no longer support you. You may arrive at a more pleasing—even wildly creative and different—arrangement, but you haven't changed the foundation or made the room any larger, and whatever problems of scale and scope you had before will still be there once you get over the novelty of your new design. To realize your full emergent potential and purpose, your starting point must be outside the room itself. Although Einstein may have used imagination as a springboard, he ultimately went beyond the mind and tapped into something deeper. In every area where humanity has taken a major leap forward, this has been the case.

A natural response to this might be, "That's not true! I can imagine myself flying in a spaceship to other galaxies, and that's something I've never experienced." But consider this: The ability to imagine otherworldly possibilities isn't necessarily transformational or evolutionary; in fact, if you study many works of science fiction, you'll see that although they have "imagined" life in the future, in many cases the protagonists are still suffering from the same problems we experience today, if not worse. No actual evolution has taken place. Imagination may take us on a journey to the edge of our known self, but for a true vision that evolves us to the next level (whether personally, professionally, or societally), we must cross the border of our conditioned mind and enter an uncharted frontier that can only be navigated through the sight of our soul.

So what is this soul-sense, this inner perceptual faculty that allows you to see and tap into true vision? It's been called many things—intuition, inner guidance, higher wisdom—but for our purposes, let's suggest a new term: Emergination. Think of it as Imagination 2.0. Whereas imagination allows you to select from your database of stored knowledge and experience to create new expressions, Emergination allows you to tap into the field of unprecedented ideas seeking to emerge, ideas beyond your experience, beyond all experience—the perfect prototypes unique to you.

If it's a better relationship your soul yearns for, activating your Emergination will make you receptive to that part of you already in love, making you a magnet for a partner who matches your soul's highest ideals. If it's a project you're working on, you can call on your Emergination to reveal the project's true essence and greater potential as well as the means to achieve these—often in ways that surprise you, stretch you, and exceed what you could have imagined. If it's a business you're trying to grow, following your Emergination will not only help you discern its next stage of evolution but also help you position it to be an evolutionary force in its industry. And unlike some manifestation techniques that focus on changing your external world, Emergination is an inside-out process that transforms you into the person you must be to handle the next phase of growth with ease, grace, and integrity.

This soul faculty of Emergination is a natural part of us, an ability anyone can develop, and something nearly everyone has experienced at one time or another. It is more readily activated in moments when you're relaxed and receptive, feeling a sense of love, gratitude, or awe or when a crisis has forced you to your knees. The mind stops, something else opens up, and you have a flash of insight or a solution to a problem without a process of deliberation. But it's not necessary to wait until you hit rock bottom or have a mountaintop moment. Through active practice, you can consciously cultivate your Emergination, ultimately making way for your vision to shine through.

Exercises

There are many ways to access this inner source of inspiration, from meditation and prayer to chanting and automatic writing. The clues to who you truly are and why you're alive are everywhere, inside and outside. The key to activating this faculty is in becoming interested in that guidance and developing a more observant, receptive, and reflective mind. Another key is a willingness to stay in a creative, nonjudgmental, childlike space—what I call the Vision Studio. This is a sacred inner environment where the editor, critic, and analyst aren't allowed, at least not until you've expressed a complete version of your vision that inspires you. The following four exercises are designed to help you in this task. To get you started, here is a simple practice to begin opening to this higher vision.

Activating Your Emergination

Close your eyes and take a few slow, deep inhalations. As you exhale, allow yourself to release all the tension in your body, all the issues of the day, and all your concerns for the future. Let go and sink into this moment. Be aware of your breath as it flows in and out, either by gently focusing your attention on your nostrils or on your rising and falling abdomen. Don't control it; allow the breath to do what it wants, sometimes breathing deeply, other times more shallowly. Just remain aware and relaxed.

As you settle in, set your intention for this exercise. It doesn't matter what goal you have, whether it's to manifest a job, find a new mate, heal your body, or make more money. The purest intention, for the purpose of this work, is to make conscious contact with your spirit, to awaken to the truth of your being. This is most effective because it seeks nothing but self-actualization and therefore carries no resistance, whereas an intention to get something seemingly separate from us pulls us back into the fundamental duality this work aims to heal.

Feel the vibration of your intention. Take a deep breath and allow that feeling to expand, filling your whole body. Then another one, allowing this energy to fill the space you're in, until you're completely enveloped in its warm glow. Release all your ideas of what should or shouldn't be. There's no right or wrong way to do this. Just trust your intuition.

With your intention firmly established, you can move to the next stage of the exercise where you prompt your higher consciousness with questions about your vision. We'll just focus on one theme for now, but you can always add to this as you become more comfortable with this exercise.

Ask yourself: What is the vision of my life? What is the divine (or highest) idea of my life? What does it look like? Feel like? What is its essence? (For "my life" you can substitute whatever you hope to gain clarity on: "my family," "my relationship," "my work." You can also ask, "What is God's idea of my life?" or "What is trying to emerge through me, and as me?")

Remain alert. Wait, watch, listen. Become aware of whatever images, sounds, or sensations arise. Sometimes what comes up will be literal. You'll see images that explicitly portray your vision in the world. Other times your experience may be more symbolic and a connection will be unclear. Some people see images in Technicolor. Others will have a more physical, sensual experience. You might only get a feeling or a vibration. Pay attention but don't judge; there's no better or worse, no right or wrong. Whatever comes up is part of the process. If you find yourself drifting—planning your grocery list, worrying about bills—gently bring your attention back to the breath. But don't be dismissive of anything. In this exercise, even seemingly external distractions might be synchronistic clues from your soul.

You can repeat the questions as many times as you like or feel is necessary in order to elicit a genuine experience. As insights come through, you can open your eyes and take notes or you can wait until after the meditation. Some people prefer to wait because opening their eyes and writing takes them out of the deep flow. Others find that if they wait, they forget what emerged, the same way dreams fade after you get up. Experiment with both ways. In any case, trust that what you need to receive and remember, you will, and that even if you don't remember, there's valuable work being done in the deeper recesses of your consciousness.

As you develop, you can add other questions or ask these basic questions in different ways. As long as your intention remains pure—to have a deeper realization of who you truly are and the vision for your life—and you practice it with some consistency, it will yield rich fruits. If you want to dive into a more in-depth version of this practice, consider exploring Michael Bernard Beckwith's powerful work *Life Visioning*.

Excavating the Soul: A Vision Workshop

For some people, the vision of their life isn't easily coaxed out. It's not because the vision isn't speaking to them; rather, that it's just been suppressed so long by rational thinking and cultural conditioning that they can't hear it anymore. This usually leads to two common questions: "How can I tell what my real vision or purpose is?" and "How can I know what my soul really wants?" And when answers begin to arise, they're often followed by another question: "Is this my spirit/intuition or my ego speaking?" The result is that we doubt the guidance, doubt ourselves, and fear making the wrong choice.

First of all, you can rarely make a wrong choice if you have the right intention. Even a wrong choice born of a sincere intention will lead you to learn and grow, strengthening your ability to listen to inner guidance and make better choices. We've been taught that the path to success is in doing all the "right things," but how many people have failed by doing all the right things and succeeded by breaking all the rules? I'm not saying that developing skills and taking thoughtful action are not important, but intention is the rudder beneath the water's surface; it's what really steers the ship.

When faced with a choice of action, instead of focusing on why you shouldn't do something, ask why you *should* (or why you want to). As you tune in to this part of yourself, you not only discover the layers of false motivation—and begin to release them—you eventually hit that soft, glowing core where the *why* turns into the *what*. You discover that the thing you're striving for, the thing that fuels your *why*, is actually the very thing you're made of. You're already it, remember? Those strong desires to go out and achieve something are actually the something in you seeking to get out. So let's take some time to dig more deeply, to go on an archeological expedition of your soul and see what's really buried there.

Desires and Goals

Let's look at your desires and goals. All the things you want to have and achieve are clues to the larger vision trying to emerge. It's not that you will necessarily get all these things or that the final picture will look the way you imagine (in fact, as you emerge, you'll discover that many of the things you thought you wanted were just decoys), but because there is only one reality, even your false desires are guiding you to a deeper truth. As you bring greater awareness to these desires, you begin to crack open the hard shell of the ego and glimpse what's inside trying to get out. Are you ready for a breakthrough?

First, create two columns on a page. On the left side, write down your desire/goal. On the right side, write down why you want it. Be honest. Start with the things you want most and work your way down. If the reason you want something is to get something else materially, add that new object to the "Desire" column and write down why you want it in the other column. For instance, if you wrote, "I want to make a million dollars," and in the "Why" column you put, "To get a house," put "To get a house" in the "Desire" column, and put why you want the house in the opposite column. Do this until you get a non-material reason in the right-hand column. For example, in terms of the house, you might put "To feel secure." You've now distilled your desire(s) to the feeling of security, which is the real goal.

Now take a look at those reasons. Why do you want what you want? Do you see a pattern? Did you attribute the same *why* to more than one entry? Are your *whys* based on what you want from others, or are they inner qualities? For example, let's say you wrote in your "Desire/Goal" column, "I want to be a successful author." Then in your "Why" column, you wrote, "So people will love and respect me." You still haven't gotten down to the real *why* at your core. This entry also belongs in the "Desire/Goal" column. Take the *whys* that depend on getting something from someone else—even if it's non-material—and put those in the "Desire/Goal" column. Then write down why you want those. Working with the entry, "I want people to love and respect me," you might put in the "Why" column, "So that I will *feel* loved and respected," or "So that I'll love and respect *myself*."

Now, *that* is a *why* you can work with.

But something else important has occurred. You started out thinking that what you wanted was to be a successful author, have fame and fortune, and gain the respect of others but discovered that what you really want is to feel loved and respected. Feeling loved and respected is an inside job! It has nothing to do with *anything* outside of you. You, and only you, have the power to generate these feelings. Generating them is your real goal and the core of your vision. (In "Stage Two: Cultivate Congruent Conditions," we'll work more specifically on activating these qualities.)

As you uncover the true motivation behind your desire to attain things, they begin to lose their luster, their irresistible pull. The more you come to understand that what you actually want is already within you, the less appeal the outer struggle has. When you understand that what you're really going for is self-love and acceptance (or whatever essential quality you may be after) and you realize you can only find this on the inside, your journey both ends and finally begins. The resistance falls away and self-love and acceptance naturally emerge.

This doesn't mean you should just stop taking action in the world. Far from it. As a matter of fact, you'll become more productive because you'll know where your good really comes from and therefore won't be blocking it by projecting it onto someone or something else. All the false desires based on false motives fall away. And what remains is the true path you're meant to walk. On this path, you'll encounter tasks and you'll have goals and a grand purpose, to be sure, but they will not be motivated by what you can *get* but rather by what you're here to *give*. From this space, knowing that you already have everything you need within you, your actions unfold from a desire to share what you have and who you are, not because you need to express yourself to feel whole but because your wholeness cannot help but express itself.

Take a look at that list again. You should have a right-hand column (your *whys*) filled with qualities you want to embody within yourself. Along the way, you'll probably also discover some desires/goals that aren't attached to getting something from someone. For example, you may have written as a desire/goal, "I want to share my gifts with the world." And in the "Why" column, you may have genuinely written, "So people can benefit from them." This is an effective motivation. It's not *created* by your ego; it's not created at all. It is your very nature announcing itself, and that nature is always about giving, shining, sharing, pouring forth that imprisoned splendor for no ulterior motive. (The only caveat to this is, if you *do* have a hidden agenda, if you look deeper and realize that the reason you want to give is to get approval, validation, or recognition, then giving isn't the real goal; activating the inner feeling of self-worth is.)

None of this is intended as a judgment on other types of motivation. There's a place for everything on the ladder of our evolution. But a motive that doesn't seek to *get* anything—a motive that is a core desire—won't perpetuate old wounds or keep you and those around you unconscious. It will have a liberating, illuminating, expanding effect on you and anyone it touches. It will also emerge free of the resistance that normally accompanies our ego's agendas.

You should now have two sets of desires/goals here. On one hand, you know the material things you're after: the new business, the new house, the increased wealth—you name it. And that's all good. But you also have a list of inner goals. And you are becoming increasingly aware that what you *really* want is primarily an inner experience, a quality of being such as self-love, confidence, security, and abundance. From this perspective, the phrase "living a quality life" takes on a whole new significance.

Let's reiterate: Laying this inner foundation for your vision is not the end; it's the beginning. Upon this spiritual foundation you'll build a house that the storms of this world will not tear down. So let's keep building.

The All-In Dream

In the initial Emergination exercise, you opened up to your deepest vision. You didn't let your ego impose its ideas on it, and perhaps you were surprised, even shocked, by what you discovered. In the past you've probably designed visions based on what you want. With Emergination, you've begun to discover the excitement of opening up to what wants you. Then through the desires and goals process, you focused on the core values seeking to emerge. Now that you're more mentally limber and receptive, we're going to let you envision, without limits, the life of your dreams. From this space, your mind is less of a creator and more of a channel for your true vision.

Take a moment now and get comfortable. Close your eyes and take a few deep, cleansing breaths. With each inhalation, imagine you are breathing light into your heart. With each exhalation, imagine you're exhaling anything that no longer serves you. Relax into this moment, releasing any concern for the future and any residue from the past.

Recall a time in your life when you felt really connected—any moment that activates a positive feeling, a vibration of love, inspiration, aliveness. Just let yourself go there. Be in it, feel it again. Then breathe, and as you exhale, let that feeling expand to fill your body with that energy.

From this greater activation and receptivity, allow yourself to open up to the highest vision of your life—not the vision you think you *should*, *could*, or *have to* live; not merely the vision you think is practical, logical, or reasonable. Give yourself permission to see and feel what you truly, deeply desire. If you knew you were totally supported and had all the resources you needed—the talents, gifts, abilities, and support—what would that vision be? Who would you be? What would you do? How would you contribute or create? Who would you support or serve? What would it look like?

Feel free to include any of the life structures—your health, wealth, work, relationships, spirituality, personal development, and service. Allow yourself to see and feel the highest possible vision. Paint the picture. See yourself doing and being in a way that truly inspires you. Hold nothing back. See people congratulating you, honoring you, praising you. Wherever you go, you meet with love and support, recognition and reward. Breathe into that and let it expand. If your self-talk starts saying things like, "Who do you think you are? How could you ever do that? That's impossible!" thank it for sharing, put it aside—lock it outside your Vision Studio—and go back to painting the vision. Remember, the *how* will kill the *what* if you let it. We're not going to allow that to happen today.

Now ask yourself, on a scale from zero to one hundred, if zero is "Somebody please put me out of my misery!" and one hundred is "OMG, I can barely stay in my body, I'm so happy!" where does this vision fall on that scale? How does this vision feel in your body right now, in this moment, when you imagine it? If it's less than one hundred, ask what it would take to raise it ten points on the scale. If it's fifty, what would it take to be a sixty, and so on? Listen and add that element to the vision. Do this until you hit one hundred, until you can't imagine a better life. If you get stuck, think about other aspects of the vision. For example, if you've been imagining your work, add the element of health or wealth or relationships until you hit one hundred. Or if you are intentionally focusing on a single area like intimate relationships, tune in to different aspects of that. This is crucial because it's easier to activate our deeper emergent resources when we have "escape velocity"—that is, a vision that lifts us out of the gravitational pull of everyday thinking—than it is to try and achieve something that only mildly revs us up. In fact, without this rocket fuel, we'll just be pulled right back down to earth.

Take a moment to journal what came up during this vision process. Pay particular attention to the qualities you were *feeling* and the qualities you were *being*. These will be very important in "Stage Two: Cultivate Congruent Conditions" as we begin activating your visionary vibration—the unique energetic signature of your vision, which is literally the substance of that vision.

Creating Your Vision Statement

The next step is to reduce your vision to a powerful statement that focuses your mind and heart on the details that matter most. This potent acknowledgment of your vision is something you can gauge everything you do against, in order to keep you on course. Without such a tool, it can be difficult to plot and stay your course. It's easy to get caught up in the daily minutiae of life, the "to-do list" mentality, only to discover when the sun goes down that you haven't accomplished anything of significance. Or you might climb the ladder of success only to discover that it's leaning against the wrong wall—or no wall at all!

To craft this powerful lodestone, which will guide you like a compass toward your True North, you'll utilize the data you've collected throughout this chapter. Let's begin.

1. Choose a few verbs that resonate, inspire, or excite you, that represent your core values. For example: to play, to serve, to build, to enlighten, to help, and so on.

2. In the context of your personal and/or professional life, decide who or what you will be engaging with or contributing to.

3. What is your ultimate goal for the people or groups you will be serving or helping? What is the value, benefit, or end result you want to create?

4. Now, take your responses from 1, 2, and 3, and combine them to create the skeleton of your Vision Statement. Once you have that, you can flesh it out using other insights you've gleaned from the explorations in this chapter.

For example:

As a writer, speaker, and teacher, I create projects that hold up a mirror to humanity, inspiring individuals to heal their past, awaken their full potential, and fulfill their destiny—creating a world that works for everyone. By conducting business with honesty, integrity, enthusiasm, and generosity, I provide a safe and productive atmosphere for people to make mistakes, take risks, create, and perform in ways that exceed their expectations, and grow in ways they never thought possible!

Your Vision Statement doesn't have to be long, but it should be clear and vivid enough to create a movie in your mind that can motivate you into action. Don't worry if you don't feel that it perfectly captures every nuance of your intention. It's something you try on, like a new coat. If after wearing it for a while it makes you itch or sweat or feel like you showed up to the party overdressed, get a new one.

You can also distill this into what I call your Emergence Mantra, a sound, word, or phrase that contains the energetic essence of your vision. It's like a reduction in cooking, where everything but what is most essential is cooked away and just one dollop of it explodes with flavor. The key is that it sums up your purpose and carries the visionary vibration. Rhonda Byrne, creator of *The Secret*, had "Bring Joy to Billions." Mine is simply "Awaken."

Think about your Vision Statement and see if you can reduce it to just a few words to form an Emergence Mantra that can take you into a deeper connection with the essence of your purpose.

Tapping into your vision and creating these navigation tools is a major step in the direction of your dreams. But it's only the beginning. What you need next is a daily practice to activate the visionary vibration and a clear plan rooted in these core values. Together, this integrates the inner and outer work into a cohesive strategy that takes you from living life by accident to living on purpose.

I've seen many lives transformed by this type of process. One individual who did this work opened up to the larger vision of her life and went from being homeless, alone, deeply depressed, and taking twenty to thirty prescription pills per day to living in her own home, getting engaged, and reducing her need for medication to just one or two pills. Had she been left to her mind's preconceived and limited beliefs of what was possible, the best she could've imagined was being pain-free and off the streets. The idea of being drug-free and married to the man of her dreams was just too far outside her self-image.

Another client was on the verge of bankruptcy, with his banker telling him he had to sell his business and home. But within a few months of tapping into the deeper vision for his life, he had more business than he could handle and launched a healing center and coaching practice, which had been his deeper calling. From where he'd started, the best he could imagine was improving his current business and getting out of debt. The possibility of actually flourishing and being a powerful healer in the world was outside his present paradigm, but it wasn't outside his potential when he opened up to that space beyond the mind.

Another person I coached through the Emergence process opened up to the energy of his vision and, in addition to healing his failing kidney, he turned his work and family life completely around. He had only hoped to heal his body, which is no small thing. But it turned out that his physical condition was an expression of a mental-emotional issue and an invitation to a deeper spiritual realization of his true nature. If you had asked him to create a vision of where his life could or should go, it never would have included the total transformation of his work and family life because his current mind-set was too contracted around his physical pain to see the greater potential and purpose beyond that.

Using this work, people have been guided to reconnect with abandoned relationships and rebuild broken families; businesses and nonprofits have developed into worldwide organizations; some who have felt truly hopeless have been inspired by profound insights and a deeper connection to the divine. When we tap into our true vision, the possibilities are endless because true vision is not something you make up; it's something *you're made of*. It's your true nature and essence, the seat of your soul, and the source of your power—beyond what the world thinks about you, beyond even what you think about yourself.

My own path has taken many unexpected but ultimately necessary turns as I've used these practices to tap into the vision. Most of the breakthroughs I've seen—both in myself and in the people I've worked with—would never have appeared on a vision board or through visualizations because they were outside the realm of our personal paradigms. Traditional manifestation techniques couldn't have created many of these outcomes because *they never could have been imagined in the first place*. In fact, in many cases, if that person had depended solely on his or her imagination, their efforts would have actually blocked the best possible results. Even more telling is the fact that, in all these cases, as my clients and I evolved to the next level, these talents and abilities no longer felt like something outside ourselves; rather, it felt like *we had discovered parts of ourselves that were there all along*. This is a common experience. As the vision emerges and takes you to new places, it doesn't feel like foreign territory; it feels like you've finally come home.

Before moving to the next section, take some time to reflect on what you've discovered. Take stock of where you are and where you want to go. Are you ready to change? I mean, really change? Remember, true change—whether in your inner world, outer world, or the world at large—requires you to go beyond your known self, beyond the stories of your life, beyond all the excuses that have held you back, and tap into that realm where your higher vision exists. The good news is that it's already here—in the same place the oak lives before it emerges through that tiny acorn. The even better news is that it doesn't matter whether you feel inadequate, lacking, or not up to the task. Just as the mighty oak emerges out of nothing but a small clump of carbon when the conditions in the soil are right, so, too, will your destiny of greatness emerge when you cultivate the soil of your soul.

Creating those conditions is what we're going to do next.

STAGE TWO

CULTIVATE CONGRUENT CONDITIONS

> You must be the change you wish to see in the world.
>
> MOHANDAS GANDHI

It was another sweltering day on L.A.'s 405 freeway—one of the busiest in the country—with bumper-to-bumper traffic covered by a layer of undulating heat waves, creating a strange shimmering junkyard that stretched as far as the eye could see. It was a miserable sight, made all the more unbearable by the gasping air-conditioner in my barely legal 1993 Camry that I had nearly driven into the ground.

"Where the hell are all these people *going*? Don't they have a life?!" I hated them. Hated them all. And not just with a detached kind of contempt. I felt personally affronted by their existence. To say I was in a bad way would be an understatement.

I wanted to lay on the horn so hard. Even though I knew it wouldn't do any good, it would have *felt* good. Instead, I started flipping through the radio stations—country, classical, oldies, indie. It was all noise. If I could just find the right song, I thought, it would drown out all the noise in my head and maybe, just maybe, I could endure this hell I was crawling through.

I finally flicked off the radio in disgust and tried to breathe and regain my composure. I was so agitated, more than usual, more than I could remember being in a long time. I felt like I was losing it. And I didn't understand why, considering all the "inner" work I had been doing lately. So I did what any self-respecting student of personal development should do when they find themselves on the verge of a nervous breakdown: I started singing "Let It Be." But not in a Beatles kind of way. It was more like a battle cry, a frustrated incantation, like I was trying to will myself into a better place. "Let it *be*, let *it* be, let it be, *let it be*, whisper words of wisdom, let it beeee!" "Let It Be" never sounded so angry (or out of tune). I sang at the top of my lungs, feeling like an ass but not giving a rip. I let myself go. I went operatic. I sang it like Freddie Mercury, then Elton John, then Bob Dylan. It was not a sound any human should *ever* be subjected to. But it took me out of my head, out of my car, out of the sweltering heat, just for a moment.

And then it happened.

A sudden dramatic shift in my awareness.

Where just a moment before I had contemplated cranking the wheel and hitting the gas, with no concern for who I steamrolled over on my way off this post-apocalyptic highway, now I was giddy with joy.

I glanced out the windshield at the impassible gridlock. What had looked like a graveyard of lost souls now looked like a work of art, a masterpiece of metal sculpture glistening with a million points of light. I looked to my left, at the car that had been my traveling companion on this journey through Dante's Inferno for the last mile and a half. The driver was staring at me like I was crazy. I gave him a wolfish Jack Nicholson grin.

I felt awesome!

The shift was so abrupt, so complete, that it stunned me into silence and sent my mind on a hunt for the cause of my sudden happiness. I reflected on my day up to this point. Did I get a surprise call with good news? No. Did I have an unexpected creative breakthrough? Nope. Did *anything* good happen? As a matter of fact, the day had been pretty unremarkable, even lousy, up to this point.

So why was I feeling so good? It couldn't just be the song. I'd sung in my car before, just as badly and with just as much gusto, but I'd never felt like my whole life was changed by it. Something profound had happened. A cosmic tumbler had clicked into place.

Cracking the Congruence Code

Looking back to that day on the freeway, there were a couple of key things that set me up for that experience of expanded awareness. The first was that in that moment, I chose to take back control of my inner reality, to attempt to feel better regardless of the outer conditions—regardless even of my mental and emotional momentum. It was from a place of desperation and frustration, and I wasn't even fully aware of it at the time. But sometimes that's the best we can do—and, as it turns out, that was good enough. The second thing was that I went out of my mind—literally. I let go, took my attention off my mental purgatory, and threw myself into the moment. In that space, a gap was created. And in that gap, the fruits of all the work I'd been doing were finally able to emerge.

This shift had really started on Sunset Boulevard a few weeks earlier. I was having lunch with a friend at some trendy spot on the strip, feeling bad about myself and my lack of work as a writer, when the coolest dude you've ever seen walked in, in his Dolce & Gabbana sunglasses, leather bomber jacket, and jeans ripped just so, to grab a to-go order. I glanced out the window, where an equally perfect blond woman waited in this guy's convertible Porsche, taking in the sun like she owned it. Mr. Cool grabbed his goods and sauntered out, looking like the happiest man alive. I half expected him to slide across the roof of his Porsche. Instead, he gave the Sun Goddess a movie-star kiss and hopped in. It was even cooler than

I'd expected—and I hated him for it. Then I swear I saw him glance up, catch me staring at him in the window, and nod with a look of *pity*—but I might've imagined that part. It felt so unfair, like the universe was rubbing my inadequacy in my face. I was hypnotized by it all, believing that his king-of-the world confidence was a result of his apparent success. He was holding the winning lottery ticket. The only ticket I had was the one I'd gotten for parking in a red zone!

Then, just like that, I received one of those cosmic kicks to the head. It dawned on me that whatever happiness I was projecting on his picture-perfect life had nothing to do with the outer picture and everything to do with the inner one. I knew that I could *feel* abundant even if my bank account wasn't, and I could feel like "somebody" even if nobody was paying attention, because my state of being was independent of my state of having. What's more, I sensed that the only thing that mattered, the thing I (and, ultimately, everyone) was really striving for was to *feel* a certain way inside, despite the ego's incessant attempts to convince us that it's the outer stuff we're after.

And feeling good was, ultimately, entirely up to me.

There was a greater peace, joy, freedom, and fulfillment in me—I was sure of that—if I could just find a way to let it out. Up to that point, I had let my outer circumstances become my master; I was still waiting for the traffic jam of my life to clear up, for the right song to play, before I would give myself permission to sing my heart out and feel what I really wanted to feel.

This line of thinking got me inspired. I knew what I had to do. I bid my friend farewell, sauntered out of the café with just a little more swagger in my step, and began what I've come to call my "inner workout routine." I would stand in front of a mirror and do a series of impassioned proclamations to activate the *feeling* that I was already the person I wanted to be. I would work myself into an affirmative high and then sit down and meditate on the buzz, bathing in it, becoming intimately aware of the *feeling tone*. (Feeling tone is an emanation of the soul that expands with awareness; emotion, on the other hand, being a byproduct of thought, tends to dissipate with relaxed attention.) I didn't force it or hold on to it. I just soaked in it. I did this every day, as well as periodically tapping back into that state amidst my daily comings and goings, in a practice I call the One-Minute Mystic (which we'll explore in a bit). I didn't have any particular goal except to create a better feeling within myself. And because the focus wasn't on external things or events, I wasn't putting much attention on how things were going in my external world, which was a good thing, since, for the most part, they weren't going that well!

I had periods of feeling good. But other than brief buzzes, I didn't notice any particularly meaningful or permanent shift—and sometimes even wondered if I was losing ground, if not my mind—until that moment in gridlocked traffic when, with every good reason to be frustrated and bored and bemoan my fate, I suddenly felt like the me I wanted to be, the me I knew deep down I really was. I had become an energetic match to my highest idea of myself—to my greater potential—and in that moment of intense stress, mixed with surrender (and a little wild abandon), the remaining resistance melted and the next level emerged.

I didn't have to do mental gymnastics to get into that zone. I was no longer affirming something. *Something* was affirming *me*. I was no longer praying. I was *being* prayed. My more expanded nature—my higher Self—was driving now; I was just a passenger along for the ride. I understood for the first time that we could be in heaven in the midst of what seemed like hell. We could be free regardless of circumstances. Most people on that freeway were in a traffic jam, but I was flying above it, no obstacles in my way. Nothing was lacking. I had no desire to be successful or rich any-more. I *was* it. It was the *feeling state*, not my outer conditions, that brought freedom and fulfillment. It lingered for a while and then *integrated* (an important word moving forward).

That experience of "leveling up," if you will, would have been sufficient. But it was just the beginning. Within a week or so, a whole new life unfolded—new opportunities, better financial circumstances, greater creativity, deeper insights. The expanded state of gratitude and interior abundance I had activated created the congruent conditions for that next stage of my evolution to emerge. As I lived more consistently in this higher vibration of joy and thanksgiving, the universe gave me even more things to be happy and thankful for.

But an even deeper truth was revealed as well.

This abundant, joyful life had been in me forever—it already *was* me. It just couldn't be expressed until I was in alignment with it. It wasn't that life had been holding anything back from me; *I* had been holding me back from life. And as I unpacked this experience more fully and began to map out the steps to achieving this new state, I was able to use it to evolve every area of my life—from having children and creating a dream home for my expanding family to growing my business from a one-room apartment to its global reach today.

I'll show you how to do the same, but before we focus on *how to do it*, it's helpful to know a little more about *how it works* so you're not going on blind faith. By understanding that it's not personal but principle, you'll be more likely to practice the principles regardless of what you think or feel about them—and create results that are consistent.

The Ecology of Consciousness

Everything we see, feel, taste, touch, every relationship we have is all happening in the mind. It's the quality of our inner landscape—the Ecology of Consciousness—that creates the conditions of our outer world. This is liberating because it puts the determining factor of our experience on us rather than anything "out there." We no longer have to accept the belief that our genes, the stars, or our past lives, among other things, have any power over us, and we can finally reclaim all the power we've given away.

The first step in developing this new awareness is understanding the reality-creating mechanism of consciousness—how the experience of the senses is an expression of mental and spiritual activity, not a reality in itself. We don't see or hear because we have eyes and ears; we have eyes and ears because seeing and hearing are aspects of consciousness. That's one reason you can experience sight and sound in your mind without the use of physical senses. And when you dream, you can experience everything as fully as you do in waking life. In fact, dreaming activates many of the same sensorial regions of the brain we use while we're awake—but we're not, because it's all a play of consciousness. So the fact that our waking world feels real doesn't necessarily make it so. Taken a step further, our body doesn't actually feel—the mind does. The phantom limb phenomenon illustrates this. When someone loses a limb, they'll sometimes still feel pain or itching in the missing limb and reach into empty space to scratch an appendage that is no longer there.

The whole world "out there" is a movie we're projecting on the screen of our mind.

If you want to fully activate the Law of Emergence and become the master of your life, you must accept that what's outside is a reflection of what's inside. This is almost a cliché in metaphysical circles, but it's rarely deeply understood or fully practiced. The fact is, we all believe, to some extent, in powers or influences outside of ourselves. We're not to blame for this perspective; we've been caught in the mass delusion that we are separate from our divine nature. But search the great spiritual teachings and you'll see that this is the core illusion they've been trying to awaken us from.

When Jesus stood before Pilate, who claimed he had the power to give him life or death, Jesus said, "You would have no power over me if it were not given to you from above,"(John 19:11) meaning divine or higher consciousness. He affirmed this divine nature as the only power. And where did he say it was? Within us. This isn't a religious statement; it's a universal spiritual principle. All power is in you. Not some of the time or in some cases, but all the time, without exception.

Life doesn't happen *to* you; it happens *through* you. If the world outside feels polluted, it's because the divine power plant within you—that energy source capable of generating anything you want—is spewing out the toxic byproducts of negative thinking. If you find yourself in broken-down conditions—whether in your body or affairs—there are neglected or abandoned places within you in need of care. If your relationships are fraught with conflict and power plays, that means that interior parts of you are in a battle for territory. Our entire planetary condition is a reflection of the ecology of human consciousness. That's why we'll never live in harmony with nature or each other until we live in harmony within ourselves.

This is a controversial topic because it seems to imply that all our problems are our fault. If we have challenges, we brought them upon ourselves. If we get sick, we created it. If we have an accident, our thinking caused it. It seems to be a "blame the victim" idea, and there's nothing worse than being down and having someone imply that it's your fault. *But this isn't about blame or judgment.* First, you didn't create the misperceptions that may be wreaking havoc in your life. They were here before you were. *It's not your fault.* We're all impacted by limited universal beliefs until we consciously reject them. Second, it's principle, not personal. The law that turns beliefs into experience doesn't discriminate between the "disempowering" or "life-giving" thoughts planted in your mind any more than the soil can discriminate between the seed of a flower or a dandelion. If you plant a rose, no matter how "bad" a person you think you are, the law grows a rose. If you plant a dandelion, no matter how "good" a person you may be, the law gives you a weed.

Just by being born, we become susceptible to all the beliefs of humanity. And these seeds of limited thought are blown about by the winds of human experience like the airborne seeds of dandelions. It's up to us to keep them off our plot of land or pluck them out when we find them there. If we don't, those seeds will become an unwelcome harvest—not because we're bad or good or unlucky but because that's just the way it works. This might sound like the universe is unfair and unfeeling, but it's designed to give us the greatest freedom. And when we understand how it really operates and learn to cultivate the soil of our soul—taking full responsibility (not blame) for everything that grows in our life—it will blossom with boundless abundance and beauty.

The Crisis of Incongruence

Once you understand that everything is an activity of consciousness and nothing external has power over you, the next principle to grasp is that your good is already broadcasting. Like radio waves, your favorite music is playing right where you are, but you can't sing to it unless you tune your dial to the station it's playing on. When you do, you don't create the music—you reveal the music *that is already playing*. It isn't in some other time or place; it's here and now. The distance between you and your music is a distance of frequency. The same is true for the song of your soul. The beat of abundance, the harmony of health, the rhythm of rich relationships—all the greatest hits are broadcasting right where you are. But just like I had to stop waiting for the right song to pull me out of that traffic jam and start singing it myself, you must stop waiting for life to play the perfect music and sing what you want to hear—like your whole life depends on it!

When we don't experience this symphony of success, it's because we're not tuned in to it within. We might be trying all manner of techniques to be healthy, wealthy, and wise, but our chronic mental, emotional, and physical habits are not in integrity with it. We're incongruent. Each morning, we may meditate and stare at our goals or vision board, aligning with that higher frequency, but then go through our day without mindfulness, which tunes us back in to the static. If we listen to the news on the way to work, we begin to vibrate with the fear-mongering. If we congregate around the coffee urn, agreeing about the struggling economy, we create a preset button for poverty consciousness. If we spend our lunch hour commiserating about all the bad people doing us wrong, we may be eating a healthy meal but what we're really ingesting are toxic judgments. And if we watch more bad news before going to sleep or don't do anything to clear away the negativities of the day, our subconscious will churn for hours, unabated, digesting all the gory details.

This is a key reason we fail to fulfill our potential: *our unconscious thoughts, feelings, words, and actions are moving in one vibrational direction while our soul is moving in another.* We're trying to serve two masters—the human belief system of fear and lack and the divine reality of love and abundance. We become a house divided, and a house divided cannot stand. The solution is to accept that *we are the only law unto our life*, and then, step by step, create a strategy that consciously and unconsciously brings our life into coherence with our highest vision. That will be the primary goal of the rest of this chapter—and ultimately this entire book.

Let's start tuning in.

The Three Steps to Congruent Conditions

No matter where you've come from or where you are, when you practice the following three steps, you can tune your consciousness in to the station where your music is playing, aligning yourself with your soul's own visionary vibration. The three steps, in brief, are:

1. Identify the three Soul Purpose Pillars of your vision: feeling, being, and doing.

2. Activate the first two Soul Purpose Pillars, feeling and being ("doing" will be addressed in-depth in the next stage).

3. Practice the Daily LIFT strategy, which stands for Living In the Feeling Tone of your vision (aka your visionary vibration).

The Three Soul Purpose Pillars

Your vision is made up of three primary pillars: how you would *feel,* who you would *be*, and what you would *do* if you were living it fully? This is an important distinction because people focus most on the doing, less on the feeling, and rarely on the being. If their vision is to have a thriving business and the love of their life, they write down what that would look like—primarily, what sorts of activities they would see themselves engaged in (the doing). They then create a plan for how to make it happen and go about trying to achieve it.

As already noted, however, even if we do manage to manifest our outer goals, we tend to bring along with us the same self-concept or, worse, our self-concept is even more damaged by the journey. Besides the fact that we haven't made ourselves congruent with what we believe we want, there's a spiritual perspective that's even more significant: *at the soul level, if you achieve something in the world but don't evolve spiritually, you've achieved nothing.* It's a non-event. In broader terms, if you go through life accomplishing only outer results without transforming your inner being, *you've lived a non-life.*

From the soul's perspective, you might as well have stayed home and sat this one out. The familiar refrain "What does it profit a man if he gains the world but loses his soul?" could be updated: "What does it profit a man if he gains the world but doesn't grow?"

At the end of the day—let alone the end of our life—it's not what we've achieved that gives us the most satisfaction; it's who we've become. Are you more peaceful, more loving, more patient, more connected to yourself and others? Do you feel more empowered and authentic in your self-expression? If you feel more in possession of yourself—even if you don't have more possessions in the world—you've had a good year. Then, through the Law of Emergence, that new state of *being* must manifest as more *having*. Interestingly, you'll discover at this point that more *having* is just icing on the cake.

Identifying the Three Soul Purpose Pillars

In this step, you'll be tapping into your vision to uncover how you would feel and who you would *be* if you were living it fully.

Pillar One: The Feeling Qualities

Take a moment to contemplate and/or visualize your ideal vision, to whatever extent you've uncovered it, and ask, "How does it *feel* to be in this ideal life? How does it feel to give, receive, have, be, and do at this level?" Enhance the vision to increase that feeling. If you're in an ideal relationship, see yourself being lavished with loving affection. If you're working at your ideal job, see yourself greeted with thanks and congratulations, hugs and handshakes. If you're in the public spotlight, see yourself getting a standing ovation, with recognition and reward everywhere you go. Don't worry about how or why; just expand the possibilities and magnify the feelings. Take a breath, take in the vision, and write down the qualities you felt.

Pillar Two: The Being Qualities

Return to the vision state and ask, "If I were living this vision fully, who would I be? How would I walk, talk, and engage others?" Close your eyes and visualize this. Notice how you move through this world, your qualities of character. Are you more empowered, confident, generous? Imagine a situation you've been struggling with and notice how you would respond differently now. Are you more centered, patient, forgiving? A being quality tends to be more active than a feeling quality. (For example, "giving" is a being quality, whereas "abundant" is a feeling quality.) Be aware of the differences between your vision and your current behaviors. Write down these qualities of being.

Activating the Soul Purpose Pillars

In this step, you'll discover the people, places, activities, and objects that help you *feel* the qualities of your vision and step more into *being* the person you would be if it were true. This allows you to begin engineering a way of life that regularly activates the visionary vibration until it becomes permanently embodied.

Activating the Feelings

Create a page with two columns. On the left, write "Feelings" (or "Qualities"), and on the right, put "Activation." Under the heading on the left, giving at least a few lines in between each, write the qualities or feelings you most wish to experience—such as happiness, affection, peace, and so forth. Then on the right, list activities, people, places, and sensory objects—such as pictures, physical items, sounds, and smells—you believe would make you feel that quality or that have done so in the past.

Let's say you have written the quality of confidence. Maybe you remember a sport or creative activity that made you feel good about yourself, but over time you stopped doing it. You might recall a supportive friend who makes you feel like you can do anything, but you don't talk often. Write that down. Perhaps you're working on peace and you feel it when you take walks, but you don't take them anymore. Or there's some music that stirs a sense of joy within you, although you rarely listen to it. You could even remember going to grandma's house and smelling freshly baked bread and recall how it made you feel safe and at home, but you've never baked bread yourself. Write it all down: the walks, the music, the baking bread.

What you're uncovering is a whole array of situations, circumstances, and individuals that activate the visionary vibration in your life and assist you in tuning in to—even *entering* into—a state that is congruent with your vision. Your homework (or rather, homeplay) is to pick one quality; then from the list you created on the right side of the page, choose an activity or two, and design them into your life. That might be making a date or maybe even a regular get-together with the friend who makes you feel good. It could be hanging some new pictures, placing some new objects on your desk, or baking a fresh loaf of sourdough. It could mean joining a gym or quilting group, signing up for yoga, or scheduling a daily walk in the woods—whatever helps you feel these positive feelings.

Start with one quality. Then choose another and introduce more of the vibration-raising activities you've listed to activate more good feelings. This isn't necessarily about adding a lot more to an already full schedule. In some cases it might involve layering on to existing activities to make them even more positive, such as exercising in the park versus the gym because being outdoors fills you with joy. Or adding certain music, aromas, or objects to your work area to enhance it. In other cases, it could be replacing one activity with a more congruent one, such as taking a walk during your lunch break instead of playing on your phone or meditating during a commercial break instead of watching the ads.

Activating the Being

Make another page with two columns. On the left, write "Being," and on the right, put "Activities." In the "Being" column, write down the qualities of being you would express if you were living your ideal vision, leaving some space between each. Whereas qualities of *feeling* are more internal and passive in nature, qualities of *being* are more active, such as "courageous," "outgoing," "spontaneous," "wild and outrageous," "loving," and so forth. In the "Activities" column, write down the actions you can take to start being that person now. To uncover this, you can close your eyes and tap back into your vision, feeling into it, sensing into this quality of being. Then ask, "What would it look like to step into being this in my life now?" As the answer arises, in whatever form—a vision, a feeling, an idea— continue to ask until you get a specific actionable piece of guidance.

For example, I had one client who was working with the quality of empowerment, and she got the guidance, "Love myself more." But that wasn't guidance yet; it was just an abstraction, a trick of the ego to make her believe she was getting useful information and making progress. When it's vague, it rarely results in new action or insight, and we end up relaxing back into old patterns. So I instructed her to engage the guidance, asking, "What would it *look* like to love myself more?" That brought up, "Take better care of myself."

That was progress, but it still wasn't specific and actionable. So she asked, "What would it *look* like to take better care of myself?" or, "How should I take better care of myself?" Then she heard, "Start exercising." Closer but still fuzzy. And fuzzy thinking leads to fuzzy outcomes. So I invited her to get more specific: "What *kind* of exercise? When? Where? How much?" She did this until her mind finally relented: "Fine! That yoga class you've been thinking about—do that three times a week!"

Now *that* was real guidance. And when she honored it, it activated the deeper sense of empowerment she was seeking. Had she left it at "love yourself more," she might have wrapped her arms around herself and called it a day!

You might be thinking that this is too much and you don't have time to design it, but the truth is, whatever your life is composed of, *you've already designed it*, however unconsciously. Most people want to be happy and healthy and to live their dreams, but out of fear or simply coping, they've unwittingly designed a strategy that is *incongruent* with what they really want. They consume media that negatively impacts them mentally and emotionally, eat food that isn't energetically or even philosophically aligned with their highest vision, become stuck in jobs they have little or no passion for, get cajoled into conversations or activities they have little or no interest in, and, lacking a clear intention, are swept out to sea in a riptide of dysfunctional trends.

Even many sincere seekers find themselves acting out some version of this. Before I knew how to consciously design my life around my highest vision, I often fell into these unconscious patterns. I would do some meditation in the morning if I had time and listen to some self-help CDs at the gym or in the car. And in some cases, I'd even carve out space to focus on my dream journal or vision board and take an action or two in the direction of my ideal life. The problem was that I had surrounded myself with people, environments, images, and energy *not* aligned with my ideal life, which led to me taking actions that were often in opposition to what I wanted to create and who I wanted to be. It was the proverbial two steps forward and three steps back. There was no consistent design. Things were going in all different directions, and I could never get any momentum.

After my spiritual opening, I got rid of all television, magazines, newspapers, videos—everything that had a negative message or energy—and cloistered myself in my apartment, reading spiritual literature, meditating, journaling, and spending time only with people who were on the same path. It was radical re-engineering; it was what I needed. At times you can make progress through incremental change; other times the inertia of old patterns is too strong. Just as a rocket needs to blast off in order to break free of Earth's gravity, sometimes more radical action is necessary to break the gravitational force of our limited identity. I'm not suggesting that you get rid of all your possessions, quit your job, and kick everyone who isn't positive out of your life. This is something each person needs to evaluate individually—what can stay, what must go, what needs adjusting, and what is actually working. But to move to the next level, you'll need to create a strategy that is in integrity with your soul.

The Daily LIFT Strategy

The core of your daily Emergence work is Living In the Feeling Tone (the vibrational quality) of your vision, or the Daily LIFT strategy. The Daily LIFT brings together all the elements you've developed so far into a routine through some simple exercises that you can incorporate into your day. As this becomes a consistent part of your life, it will cut a new subjective groove in your consciousness, integrating this higher frequency until it becomes a new set point, creating the congruent conditions for the emergence of your next stage of evolution.

Are you ready for liftoff?

The "Visualization-Vibration-Radiation" Process

This foundational meditation activates, expands, and integrates your visionary vibration—the signature feeling tone of your vision. You start by visualizing your ideal outcomes, really allowing yourself to get into the feeling of it. Visualizing is a skill that gets stronger with practice, so if it's difficult for you, begin by "thinking" the images and ideas and letting those thoughts generate the feelings.

As you feel your connection with the energy of your visualization, take a few deep breaths, and with each exhalation, imagine it expanding to fill your heart, your chest, your body, and your surrounding environment.

When you feel energetically expanded, hold your hands up in front of you, palms facing outward. Imagine Earth as the size of a baseball in front of you and radiate this energy to the planet, seeing it saturate every person, every creature, every river, ocean, and the land in between. As you feel or imagine this life force coursing through your heart, down your arms, and out of your hands, add a prayer, such as, *May all beings, all creatures, and all of creation be blessed unconditionally. May everyone be/have* (fill in the qualities you want to experience more in your life). *May every being, every creature, and all of creation awaken and be liberated.* Use whatever words move you, as long as they have a similar intent.

Continue to silently repeat this prayer, feeling the energy channel through you to the world, including everyone in your life—especially anyone you have a negative feeling toward. Offer forgiveness or ask for forgiveness as you radiate this energy. If you feel resistance, imagine your "resistant self" in your mind's eye and radiate this unconditional blessing to that self. Then return to the process. As the energy flows through you, imagine it uprooting any limiting thoughts, negative images, destructive memories, or old toxic energy—all of which flows out of you, dissolving into the stream of energy.

When you're ready, turn your palms back toward you and confer this same blessing upon yourself. Finally, place your hands on your heart and affirm yourself like never before, saying all the things you would love to hear—loving yourself up!

The One-Minute Mystic

Meditation is one of the most powerful spiritual tools for connecting with the God of your being and cultivating the conditions for your Emergence. Admittedly, however, it's a stumbling block for many. For the new initiate, sitting in meditation can be a frustrating or even painful experience. Even for those already on the path, there's sometimes still resistance to meditating regularly. But meditation doesn't need to be a chore, and it doesn't matter which particular technique you use to move beyond the mind and touch the timeless dimension of being.

There are as many paths to this deeper dimension as there are people. When it comes to cultivating congruent conditions, the continuity of your connection is more important than the quantity of time you spend in any given sitting. In other words, you could meditate for a long time in the morning and then be shaken by some news headline or life event that leaves you disconnected for the rest of the day. But by tapping back in more often, just long enough to get centered again, you can accelerate your progress.

I call this the One-Minute Mystic because by using simple one-minute sessions during the day, you strengthen focus, lengthen attention, dissolve blocks, and increase connection. These "mystical minutes" can be used to contemplate your vision's core qualities,

affirm your higher nature, or relax into a state of "it's already done"—
which is, after all, the underlying truth of Emergence. But be
warned, this is deceptively simple; this is not about ego, which tends
to require complex processes to make it feel important. When you
use this practice regularly—which is the key to its effectiveness—it
will create a deep shift in consciousness.

Some Daily Mystical Minutes

• Before you get out of bed, take a minute to connect with your
breath. Just observe it moving in and out. If your mind begins
to chatter, tell it you'll be with it shortly, and then bring attention back to the breath. Instead of, "Good God, it's morning!"
try, "Good morning, God." Give thanks for everything in your
life . . . then put your feet on the floor.

• Anytime you bathe or shower, take a minute to notice the water
against your skin, the sensations, the sounds. Stay in your
body, in the present moment, instead of drifting into the future
to make plans or into the past to fantasize that you won that
argument. As your body is cleansed, affirm that the mental-
emotional debris is washing away as well.

• At meals, take a minute to appreciate the aromas and flavors
of your food, and give thanks that it's fueling your body. For
a longer contemplation, consider the origins of your meal, its
progress to your table. Those ingredients were probably gathered on a farm, delivered by a truck driver, stocked by a grocer.
Further back, seeds may have been planted, grain harvested,
animals fed. The labor of many people went into making that
meal possible, not to mention the sun, rain, and the whole cosmic dance.

- Whenever you're driving (or on mass transit), when you reach a stop, take a minute to watch your breath and give thanks for the harmony of the universe and how it's reflected in the way the traffic lights, streets, and subways create order in the chaos. (When you think about the organization required to manage the massive flow of people and traffic, it's miraculous we ever get anywhere!) Then affirm that this same order and harmony is governing your life and vision.

- Before you start work (in your office or at home), take a minute to give thanks for your job, bless everyone that's part of it and everyone it touches on the planet, and set an intention that this will be the best day of your life. If you're not employed, give thanks for the abilities you have and the extra time for contemplation and connection with loved ones. If negativity arises, simply notice it and then return your focus to what you're grateful for. This cultivates abundance.

- When you use the restroom, take a minute to give thanks for how your body eliminates what no longer serves—and affirm that your heart and mind are doing the same. If you're experiencing an illness or having physical problems, focus on a healthy area. Feel the well-being there. Give thanks. This cultivates the conditions for greater health.

- If you watch television, pause during commercial breaks, mute the sound, and reconnect. Market *your* life-enhancing ideas to your mind, rather than letting someone else market their ideas to you.

- Every hour or so throughout your day, stop for one minute to check in, breathe, reconnect, and give thanks for life, and then go back to what you were engaged in. This is the foundational practice of the One-Minute Mystic. If you do nothing else, this exercise alone will have a significant impact.

• As you fall asleep, affirm that your mind and body are renewed while you rest and that you will awaken more inspired than ever before.

Becoming a One-Minute Mystic may at first feel mechanical and require discipline. But after a while, you'll notice yourself turning within automatically—even with your eyes open, in the midst of a conversation or activity. The key is consistency. As you stop, for just a minute, several times throughout your busy schedule, you'll not only have more energy and creativity but you'll also create new neural pathways that ultimately allow you to feel centered, tapped in, and turned on all day long.

3-D Affirmations

Affirmations help us recondition the limiting beliefs we hold about ourselves. The problem is, most of us have approached affirmations in a flat, one-dimensional way, while our beliefs have been laid down in a multidimensional, even holographic, pattern. Because impressions come to us in first, second, and third person (meaning, not only in "I am" terms but also "you are" and "he/she is"), they are imprinted that way in our subconscious. So it can be helpful to layer our affirmations the same way. If your affirmation is "I am a powerful, wealthy, confident person!" you could also state it as "You, [name], are a powerful, wealthy, confident person!" Then say it as "[Your name] is a powerful, wealthy, confident person!"

To implement this, you can take the feeling tones and qualities of character you wrote down in the three Soul Purpose Pillars exercise and turn each into a 3-D affirmation by stating it in all three ways. Pick one to three qualities to begin with, rather than trying to affirm all at once. Work on each affirmation until you experience some integration, until it starts to feel like that quality is an active part of your emotional-vibrational field.

Practice your 3-D affirmations while standing in front of a mirror so you can say them to yourself while looking yourself in the eye. As any limiting self-talk comes up, write it down and then go back to the affirmations. (You can turn that negative chatter into a positive affirmation later.) Start by methodically repeating your affirmations in first, second, and third person, repeating these over and over. Then as the energy builds, feel free to mix it up. You might go from first person to third person to second person and then back to third person. Trust the process. As you get comfortable, see if other affirmations or variations want to emerge.

For instance, "I'm a powerful, abundant person" could organically shift into "I'm a powerful, abundant, *gorgeous* person" and even "I'm a powerful, abundant, gorgeous, *sexy genius!*" Hold nothing back. Then at the height of the experience, when you're really buzzing, sit down and meditate on that feeling for at least a few minutes—longer, if you want. Let it soak in. Then ask, "From this energy, what am I called to release or embrace to step more fully into my vision?" Listen. See if there is any guidance playing on this station. If the message is vague, keep asking until you get something specific. Write it down. And as it feels appropriate, integrate the guidance into your Daily LIFT strategy.

If standing in front of the mirror isn't your thing, try to get over your discomfort and do it anyway. I know it can feel awkward and foolish, but that's just ego chatter, self-judgment, and protective walls you've built around your heart. If you can work through your defensiveness, you'll see the walls crumble and feel your heart open. If you want to change it up from time to time, try saying your affirmations while walking or jogging. The rhythm of your body can help you fall into a nice cadence that supports the affirmations. And the kinetic energy can help ground and activate the feelings within you even more effectively.

The Night Pages

This journaling exercise is best done at the end of the day, as an inventory of your progress. Writing down what you are noticing and experiencing helps you expand your consciousness of confidence, possibility, and overall abundance and creates the inner conditions for greater insight, inspiration, and expansion. Don't be fooled by its simplicity or familiarity. I've seen people do this work and experience spontaneous opportunities and increased prosperity in their life.

Make four lists:

• I Have

• I Can/I Am Able

• I Have Achieved/Successes

• I Am Grateful For

Under "I Have," write everything you have, inside and out; the qualities you are activating and expressing; the gifts, talents, and abilities; the people and things in your life; whatever money you have (even if it seems little). Include things you have access to that you don't actually own. You might have paved roads, sewer systems, a library system, and the Internet. All told, you probably have more wealth than some of the royalty from ancient times. Allow yourself to revel in all you have. If there's a particular area in your life where you've been looking for a breakthrough, pay special attention there and be as thorough as you can in recording all you have in that area. For example, if you want to start a business but need a million dollars in capital, the tendency is to focus on what you don't have, what's missing, and then react from that, which tends to magnify the feeling of lack and create resistance. Instead, focus on what you do have, inside and out.

Under "I Can/I Am Able," write about all the things you can do, all the things you are *able* to do. This is especially important to do in areas where you feel stuck, victimized, lacking, or inadequate. Using the example of trying to start a business, think about what you *can* do. You can create a business plan; you can call everyone you know and offer them an investment; you can learn about people who have built businesses from nothing; you can do inner work on building the mind-set of a successful business owner—there's so much you *can* do.

For the "I Have Achieved/Successes" list, write down all the things you've accomplished or achieved. Then, daily, write down at least five successes you had that day, even if it's just "got out of bed" or "brushed my teeth." There are many people who didn't achieve either of those. Again, pay attention to any area in which you're try-ing to have a breakthrough. If it's money, look for the things you've achieved in that area, including any money you've made, saved, invested, given, or found—even if it's just a penny! The universal law doesn't know quantity, just quality.

For "I Am Grateful For," it's pretty obvious. But stretch. Find things to be grateful for that you've taken for granted. Let yourself be surprised by what you find to be grateful for. Really allow thanks-giving to be activated. "I'm grateful for that person who opened the door for me." "I'm grateful for the sun activating my vitamin D." "I'm grateful for my ability to be grateful!" Once again, pay particu-lar attention to any area where you're working for a breakthrough. What can you be grateful for there?

As you do this, you're creating conditions congruent to your vision—welcoming conditions. Wealth can't come into a consciousness or experience that isn't a vibration of wealth. Nor can love take up residence where anger, resentment, or blame are making their bed. The vision that's trying to emerge is literally *made out of these qualities* you're activating.

From Anticipation to Participation: Closing Thoughts on Creating Congruence

One of the greatest shifts that happens in our consciousness as we work on cultivating the congruent conditions for our Emergence is that we move from anticipation of future good, fear of future bad, or resistance to current conditions to a greater *participation* in the spiritual good that's always here, awaiting our recognition. Remember the radio analogy. Your favorite music isn't playing in the future or in the distance; it's already here and now. And no matter how much static is on the current station—no matter what your current mental, emotional, or physical state—you can always tune in to this higher frequency.

You don't have to wait for things to get better; you're not at the whim of some external power or circumstance, because it's always within your power to *choose another station*. That's what happened to me when I suddenly found myself in heaven, despite being stuck on that highway to hell.

For thousands of years, the world has prayed to a far-off God or used all kinds of techniques to get something or make something happen when everything has been here all along. God has done all God's going to do. The work is complete. The music is broadcasting. *But you must be tuned in to receive it.* That's why so many prayers go unanswered, so many affirmations fall flat, and so many practices fail—or make things worse. People are doing all these things to get something they don't think they have—and by the very law they're setting in motion, it must reflect back more lack, limitation, and separation. *This is one of the greatest secrets.* That's why I keep repeating it. You're already in Heaven—whole, complete, and abundant—but you must cultivate the conditions congruent with that truth in order to experience it.

Master this principle, and you'll be singing a whole new song.

STAGE THREE

CREATE THE
QUANTUM PLAN

Every new beginning comes from some other beginning's end.

SENECA

A desire path (or a desire line) is a noteworthy phenomenon. It's a footpath worn thin by travelers as they find the best route to a desired place. I learned of it from an apocryphal story describing an incident on the creation of such paths. Whether or not the incident actually happened is unimportant. Like any great story, it's the truth it illuminates that moves us.

In this story, there was a university with several quads and public spaces that over many years had fallen into disorder. Brambles choked the hedgerows, and bald spots joined up like merging sunspots across the lawns, spreading from a multitude of paths created by students as they hurried along the best routes from class to class. The board of the university, feeling that the grounds didn't reflect the quality of the school, went to a renowned landscape architect to create a campus that would speak to the excellence of the school's academics and the heights of its students' achievements.

The board wanted the work done quickly, before the start of the next semester. The architect assessed the grounds and agreed to the time constraints, under the condition that he could create a design based on the school's true character and personality and would be given the freedom to move forward even if the board didn't fully understand his plan or approach. Such was his notorious reputation. But his work spoke for itself. So the board complied.

The architect wandered the campus, taking notes and sketching, paying attention to the dips and hills and how the buildings were fitted into the spaces created therein. For him, the natural lay of the land, its weathered patterns, and the lines that cut through it all told a story. His job was simply to interpret it. And by the end of the day, he knew what the campus would look like when it was done. He drew up the plans for re-landscaping and submitted them to the board for approval.

There was only one glaring omission: he hadn't included any footpaths.

The administration didn't understand his plan and resisted the idea at first, fearing that people would get lost, take all manner of shortcuts, create a maze of different routes with no order, and once again destroy the existing terrain. What's more, they were sure that they would receive many complaints about people having to trudge through dirt and mud as they stumbled their way to classes. It would be chaos.

The architect reminded them that previous experience had proven that people take shortcuts and create their own paths *anyway*, often leading to redesign, repaving, and increased expense. This time, however, they would identify the right paths and pave accordingly. Following some debate, the board relented and gave the designer a short time to prove his theory.

After a few weeks, the results weren't good.

As the board had feared, the students did appear to be creating all manner of arbitrary routes. The grounds were in disarray, and the complaints were pouring in. The architect urged the planners to trust him. Finding the true path takes time and patience, he explained, but the result would save time and money and create the optimal path—the desire path—which reflects a greater congruence with the surroundings, flows better with the natural gradient and weather, and gets people where they want to go in the quickest, most efficient manner.

Again, the school administration gave in and gave more time.

By the end of the semester, clear and distinct paths had emerged out of the chaos of choices, paths they couldn't have predicted but that more elegantly and effectively served their purpose. The pavement was laid. The landscape architect moved on, and the paths remain to this day.

The Planning Paradox

One problem with traditional planning is that it often comes from our limited mind-set and historical perspective. We plan based on what we think we want and how we *think* it should be done. But just as landscapers can't predict the best path for people to take in an area they haven't yet walked, it's difficult to plan a life—to predict where we should go and the best way to get there—if we haven't been there yet. What's more, in true Emergence fashion, the person doing the planning will not be the same person when the vision unfolds, just as the caterpillar is no longer there when the butterfly spreads its wings. The perspective, needs, and desires of a butterfly arise from a whole new world of possibility, beyond what the caterpillar could have ever conceived.

The same is true as we emerge. So how can we plan for a life we can't imagine?

This is the planning paradox.

We might visualize a superficial picture of our future, but the path that ultimately emerges out of the chaos of transformation is outside our knowledge and is rarely what we expect. Like a butterfly, our future self will see the world from a higher vantage point, which will color what we want, how we move forward, what shortcuts we're now able to take, and where we land.

What's more, most planning approaches, even more enlightened ones, are still based on the Newtonian model of life that says we are lacking and have to create plans in order to make something happen, versus the Emergence model, where we are planning in order to make the "something," which is *already* happening, welcome. Unless we understand that we already have it and it's already happening (spiritually or energetically speaking), we will start out off-course, deficient in our self-concept, and, by the Law of Attraction, manifest limitation no matter how well we plan our work or work our plan. This often leads to more complex planning methods to compensate for any error until, in frustration, we give up on the whole thing.

But fear not; complexity is not necessary!

Quantum planning is aligned with nature, putting the heavy lifting on the Emergence principle, not on the person, which allows for complex patterns to be executed with elegance and efficiency.

"To Be or Not to Be?" *That* Is the (Planning) Question

What makes this planning "quantum" is that it's not about achieving any more than the acorn must achieve an oak; it's about creating a life structure that mirrors our soul's blueprint (our divine desire path) and supports its emergence—like the structure a gardener puts around a young plant to hold it up, give it shape, and help it grow. In physics, the word "quantum" refers to the minimum amount of any physical entity involved in an interaction. In quantum mechanics, "quantum" is used to describe the fundamental framework for understanding nature at its most essential. In other words, it is our core essence in action. When we align with this core and plan from that level, we arrive at our destination before we take the first step.

What's more, a quantum plan is more concerned with *who* is trying to emerge than with *what* is externally accomplished. It's designed to accelerate your evolution, to pull more of the real you out. If the end goal of your plan doesn't require you to change, to become more of yourself, it's not a quantum plan; it's just a plan. There's nothing wrong with that, but it's not Emergence. Planning through the lens of Emergence—indeed, doing everything through the lens of Emergence—is about, well, emerging! It must bring more of your infinite potential to the surface. Because the soul is already filled to overflow, its only desire is to bring forth more of its *being* (remember your work in Stage Two on *being*?)—more life, more light, more love, and more beauty in a unique, unrepeatable way.

This doesn't mean you don't create plans that have all the traditional components—daily, monthly, yearly goals and schedules. Until you're so intimately at one with the divine design that there's no sense of separation from it, you'll often still need a plan to get things done in this world. But from the Emergence model, it will be a plan created from the inside out so that you gain not just greater possessions but greater possession of yourself. Rather than using your power to claim more of this world, your quantum plan will help you use this world to reclaim your power.

Quantum planning is about designing *a way of life* in alignment with your highest vision and building a path for it to unfold with ease. It allows you to plan as if you are doing the work but live as if God is.

The Best Year of Your Life

What if the next year could be the best year of your life? What if you could design every year so that it is better than the last? It's possible. But it will require commitment, not just interest. Remember, the ego's agenda is to keep you the same while giving you the illusion that you're growing—or that you can't grow—so there's a natural resistance that comes up when you get serious about change.

You may be afraid to commit your vision to paper. After all, what if it's too big and you're not ready for it? If it's a real vision, it *is* too big and you *aren't* ready for it—because the purpose of a vision (and its component goals) is to cause more of you to emerge. A real vision is beyond your present paradigm, so it will, by definition, feel bigger than you—just like becoming an oak would feel impossible to the acorn. Maybe you're afraid you'll commit to it and it'll change. If it's a real vision, it *will* change. (Or more accurately, your awareness of it will grow; the vision itself is an infinite, perfect, changeless pattern that becomes progressively clearer as you awaken.) Like the example of the desire path, you can't always see what's to come, because it's never happened before; it's beyond your imagination. Even if the caterpillar *could* imagine what it's like to be a butterfly, it wouldn't actually *know* because it has never left the ground.

Most of my biggest shifts and turns along the path were *not* part of my plan, nothing I foresaw. But it was because I had a vision and plan—then followed it—that I was in the position for the shift that led me to the next stage of my Emergence. So commit *something* to paper, knowing it can change and grow. It's a living, breathing document. Faith without work is dead. Action is the truest affirmation. And creating the actual documents of your vision and plan are powerful steps in cultivating the congruent conditions for your vision to emerge.

Your One-Year Vision Statement

Many people have dreams but don't know what it will take to achieve them. We often create such unrealistic expectations that we set ourselves up to fail. I've had clients who had the goal of having a hit movie in a year, not realizing that most movies take years to get made, or having a bestseller in a year, not understanding that traditional publishing takes about eighteen months, or making millions in a year when they were barely scraping by. I'm not saying that these goals aren't possible. I've helped clients go from being nearly broke to having more business than they'd ever imagined, all in a matter of months, and I know authors who have created bestsellers in a fraction of the normal time through self-publishing or nontraditional avenues of exposure. It's about knowing what you're in for and what you're up for.

In Stage One, we created a Vision Statement that reflected the more general, overall design of both your vision and your soul. Now let's explore what that divine design looks like in worldly, practical, goal-based parameters that we can fulfill on both subjective (feeling, being) and objective (doing) terms.

Before you create your One-Year Vision Statement, there are a few more steps. First, look at your life's vision and imagine how much you are inspired to accomplish toward that vision one year from now. This requires you to get more specific. This is where objective planning comes into play (which we will explore in more depth shortly, along with subjective planning). If your life vision is to be a doctor, build a school in Africa, start a clothing business, be an Oscar-winning actress, or maybe own your own home, earn a higher-education degree, or have a family, what's your timeline for that? Is it a ten-year or five-year vision? What would it look like one year from now? In other words, where would you have to be in one year to be on track for the bigger vision?

You may not know the answer. You might have to guess or do research, and that's okay—better than okay; it's half the fun! Anything that expands your awareness of the vision keeps you moving in the right direction. You want to set goals that are a stretch but not so much that your mind won't engage them. Just remember, in the Emergence model, the purpose of goal setting is not to get more from "out there" but to pull more of what's inside out. You may have to walk your desire path for a while before the best route becomes clear.

You may have heard of the classic SMART goal system,[1] a helpful tool for making your goals more achievable. SMART stands for Specific, Measurable, Attainable, Realistic, and Time-based. This is not about limitation; it's about structure. When it comes to the big vision, shoot for the stars and be open to the impossible dream (and do the LIFT process so that you're living in that high vibration where miracles can happen). But when it comes to setting goals and planning their achievement, you want to create success patterns, not failure patterns, which is what people often do when they set goals that have no relationship to their present reality.

Most people overestimate what they can do in a year and underestimate what they can do in a lifetime. Have a big life vision, but create yearly goals that you *really* intend to reach. Look at goals as commitments, as giving yourself your word. Your integrity is on the line here. This isn't a wish list you're *hoping* will happen; this is a definite vision *you're committed to fulfilling*. It's the difference between having an interest in something and being committed. Like a bacon-and-eggs breakfast, the chicken had an interest in it, but the pig was committed!

To create a target goal that is both realistic and a stretch, a goal you're willing to put your integrity on the line for, find that version of the vision that starts to make you nervous but doesn't make you want to give up before you start. For example, if you currently make fifty thousand a year and your goal is to make a million, ask yourself what amount less than a million would still feel aligned with your vision. Keep stepping it back until you get a number that *doesn't* inspire you, and then move it up until you feel that tingling sensation of inspiration and the first beads of perspiration. If the idea of making sixty thousand a year makes you sad and disappointed but a hundred thousand gets you excited, a hundred thousand is a good stretch goal for the year—as part of a five-year goal to reach a million (by doubling it every year).

The same principle applies to your subjective goals. If the subjective goal is to become an enlightened master, it's probably not a good one-year target. While I applaud your enthusiasm, cut yourself some slack and break that lifetime goal into its component parts. For example, what are some of the qualities of a more enlightened being? How about starting there? Also remember that these subjective goals are tied to who you would be if you were living your objective vision. So if your big vision has you making six figures, in love with your soul mate, or finishing a draft of the next great novel, who would you *be* if that came true? That's the quality of being you're targeting for the subjective part of your quantum plan.

Once you have a sense of your one-year goal, objective and subjective, the next step is to create a clear picture of the moment in which you'll *know* you have achieved it—the evidentiary moment. For example, if your goal is to earn a hundred thousand dollars, maybe you're looking at your year-end pay stub or bank statement showing the total income. If the goal is to build a six-figure consulting practice, maybe you're looking at your schedule and seeing enough clients booked to earn ten thousand a month. Once you're clear about the *doing/having* part of the vision, home in on the *being/feeling* part. So you're not just seeing the bank statement but you're also seeing yourself relaxing in your office or by the pool, enjoying your life, feeling at peace, and radiating confidence.

If possible, be even more specific. For example, if presently you tend to get angry in traffic or irritated by your children, ask, "How would I be in these situations if I embodied my one-year goal of being?" The outcome you imagine will one day be the evidence that you've achieved the goal. Then you integrate that imagining into your vision. This practice is not about becoming rigid or attached to an outcome, because the truth is we don't know how things will ultimately look. Rather, it's about establishing something concrete in our

mind, something we can commit to and generate a visionary vibration around. Otherwise the ego will try to keep your goals vague and
touchy-feely and your results will be equally amorphous that no real
change will likely take place. The key with this exercise is to include
all three Soul Purpose Pillars—feeling, being, and doing.

Once you have imagined your evidentiary moment, expand
from there to get a glimpse of what the rest of your life will look
like from that new level. What are you expressing in all the core
dimensions of your life—health, wealth, work, relationships, personal development, spirituality, and service?

Take some time now to get in touch with this evidentiary
moment, the image that most vividly illustrates your fulfillment
of the one-year vision. Then unpack the rest of these core dimensions until you have a detailed description of your one-year vision.
Finally, write it out as a one-page affirmative Vision Statement in
the present tense. For example:

> "It's January 2016, and I'm standing on the veranda of my Ital-
> ian villa, sipping wine with my soul mate. We're so in love I
> can barely describe it. I've just finished my latest book . . ."

Take time to really enjoy the writing of this. Let your heart and
soul speak on the page. If you need to put on some music and dance
or sing to activate the energy, go for it. You can do this for your five-
year vision as well, but the one-year is the working document we'll
be using. To ensure that you don't create limitations, you can add to
the end of this statement: "I accept this, or something better, for the
highest good of all concerned."

The Quantum Plan

A plan without vision often results in mediocrity or perpetuates the
status quo. But a vision without a plan is wishful thinking. Having a

vision without a plan is like having a destination without a map or a means to get there. It's just a nice idea. If it's strong enough, it might eventually inspire you to move toward it, just as evolution eventually brought us to the point of being upright, thinking creatures. But you don't want to wait another ten million years to let the natural course of evolution pull you along in its tide. We've evolved to a place where we must cocreate with the evolutionary impulse in order to fulfill our destiny; we must stop believing that the world is happening to us and realize that we are happening to the world.

The Objective Side

The objective side of your quantum plan is the doing and achieving—the part we're most familiar with. If you've been following along and doing the work so far, you've developed a sense of your life's vision. Maybe you have even started thinking about how to fulfill it. However, if you're like most people, that's where things get a little sticky—and by sticky, I mean we feel stuck. We start wondering how we're going to get from here to there—or we imagine being there and try working back to here—but there are so many potholes and blind spots, dark alleys and dead ends that we stop planning or never really start. The assumption is that we should have all the answers *before* we start planning, rather than understanding that the main reason to plan, from the Emergence model's point of view, is *because* of all the unknowns.

It's only natural to have a plan with gaps. The gaps are gifts. The gaps show you where you can learn and grow, where more of you is trying to emerge, and give you a focus for research. So as you plan, be sure to give some focus to these "holes." When we don't *consciously identify what we don't know*, that ignorance remains unconscious and can manifest as anxiety, procrastination, and all manner of self-sabotage. This can lead to feeling unworthy, believing it's not meant to be, or thinking that we're just messed up. The truth is that in alerting us to our lack of clarity and direction, our unconscious is actually trying to protect us.

When you are aware of the holes, you can welcome them, and they'll open up new adventures, guiding you to discover and study people who have done what you want to do so you can learn from what they did, avoid the mistakes they made, and fill in the missing pieces—maybe even make new discoveries. If you don't know how to do something, instead of saying, "I don't know how to do it," and giving up, make finding out how to do it part of your plan. That kind of thinking will make it impossible to become stuck and, over time, will create its own momentum. Every time you hit a gap, you'll know it means you have to learn something new. Ask empowering questions: "Where can I learn how to do this? Who does this well that I can learn from, or who might be able to direct me to someone who does?" Then you'll *include* those learning experiences in your plan and put them on your calendar. This framework will not only make you smarter and stronger; it'll make you unstoppable.

One other note about creating your objective plan: at most, tackle only a few major focuses. If you're trying to do too many things, you'll be less likely to do any of them—or at least do them well. The last thing some of us want to hear is that we have to choose, but we do. That doesn't mean you won't do more or eventually do everything you want, but if you study successful people who have created real-world (and world-class) results, you'll find that, at least initially, they picked a focus and followed through.

The Subjective Side

As we've touched on already, one key difference between a quantum plan and more traditional plans is that the quantum plan is designed from the inside out. It's as much about who you plan to *be* as what you plan to do. The subjective side of the quantum plan is focused on achieving an inner state, because if you don't have the inner plan aligned, the outer plan won't get you where you need to go, even if you get where you thought you were supposed to. It's about evolving, letting the larger, more refined *you* come out to play. That's what your soul cares about and what your soul purpose is designed to do. You'll have the byproducts, the fun external stuff, but who you become, how you deepen and enrich yourself and others mentally, emotionally, and spiritually—that's what makes for a great day, the best year, and an extraordinary life.

In the subjective part of the quantum plan, we return to the Soul Purpose Pillars of *feeling* and *being*, and the specific qualities you came up with in the three Soul Purpose Pillars exercises. If you did those exercises, you've identified the qualities of character you imagine you would be expressing and the feelings you would be experiencing if you were living your ideal vision. You should also have a list of activities you believe will generate these feelings and allow you to step more into this next state of becoming. These will become part of your plan. If you haven't done these exercises, I encourage you to do so. *Don't skip this part of the process.* The whole Emergence model rests on the idea that life happens *through* you, not *to* you. If real change doesn't occur on the inside—if you try to change the world but remain the same—that's not Emergence; that's business as usual. And if your intention is to live your soul's purpose and highest potential, your inner life has to be as much a part of your plan as your outer world.

Creating the Plan

To create your quantum plan, take your One-Year Vision Statement and work backward from each of your one-year goals to the first step you must take to accomplish them. If you have a five-year vision, you can use this same process to break it down to your one-year vision and goals first. Let's say your goal is to start a business. Before you accomplish that, you will need to secure a location for your business or build one—either online or in the world of bricks and mortar. Before that, you will need to create or purchase whatever inventory you will be selling and possibly hire staff. Before that, you will need to secure the financing to pay for this venture. Before that, you might need a business plan and marketing strategy. And before that, you might have to research the type of business you want to start, identify the most successful players in your field and what they do that works and what they're not doing that you could implement.

Do this until you reverse-emergineer your way back to the present moment. Repeat this process for each objective goal. Then do the same for your subjective goals. And remember, it's okay if there are gaps and questions. To help you organize the plan, I suggest breaking it down into the four quarters of the year and identifying what would need to be accomplished by the end of each quarter to keep you on track for the next one.

The Greatest Day of Your Life

"This is the day the Lord has made. Let us rejoice and be glad in it," reads Psalm 118:24. Metaphysically speaking, "Lord" means "the great law of life." This statement is a reminder of the principle that this day, like this year, as we spoke about earlier, is a perfect idea in the divine mind, and the way to experience that innate harmony and boundless possibility is to "rejoice and be glad" in it. In Emergence, this means having a daily strategy that keeps us congruent with our highest vision—*feeling* the visionary vibration alive within us—so that we can allow the greatest day of our life to emerge. Day after day.

Impossible? No. Will you achieve it every day? Unlikely. But if you accomplished it even a couple of days a week, wouldn't it be worth the effort?

So while you are focusing on all the practical steps, keep foremost in mind that the Greatest Day of Your Life—indeed, the whole Emergence model—is about creating a *way of life* in line with your soul's essence and purpose. This means making it a top priority that what you think about, talk about, focus on, and do are in alignment with who you *really* are and intend to be. If you follow that, even if you don't do everything "right," you'll still progress. As the old metaphysical axiom states, he who is wrong in mind can do all the right things but it will still turn out wrong; but she who is right in mind can do all the wrong things and it will still turn out right.

Because we've already covered many of the congruence practices in the Daily LIFT strategy, in this section we'll be focusing on the practical structure of your day—how to prioritize it, manage it, and engage it to activate and express what matters most.

A common approach for deciding what to put first is the ABC model: (A) something bad will happen if it doesn't get done, (B) something good will happen if it gets done, or (C) it would be nice if it got done. Category A could be a project that is due today or you'll get fired or lose the account, a past-due bill that must be paid, or anything you've already been hired or paid to show up for. The B category might be turning in a proposal for a job you've been offered, going on an important date, writing the next five pages in your book, making sales calls, meditating, going to the gym, and so on. And a C would be things like having lunch with a friend, going to the movies, or investigating an interesting project or potential partnership you might like to pursue but isn't connected to your immediate goals. This doesn't mean you never do things like have lunch with a friend; in fact, if these are part of your Daily LIFT practice or if you have a top priority to build a relationship with someone, they might fall under the B category.

You could also have a category that allows for more long-term planning of these priorities: something bad will *eventually/most likely* happen; something good will *eventually/most likely* happen. Most of these will be taken care of if you've worked out your plan and are continuously revising it. Sometimes, however, there are good and bad things on the horizon you need to deal with, but they're not urgent yet (for example, that scheduling email you need to get out to your clients before the end of the month or your schedule will become unmanageable or that proposal for a possible job that isn't due right away).

If you know you are someone who has a tendency to get distracted and not accomplish what you'd intended, consider looking at your day and asking yourself: "What is the one thing I *must* do today, the absence of which would make this day feel incomplete?" Then *do that first*. Many of us look at our list of to-dos and do the easiest ones first. It gives us a sense of momentum and accomplishment, and sometimes that can be a helpful strategy if we're feeling stuck. But if you're always leaving the toughest task for later and often not getting to it, this tactic could be creating the illusion of productivity and hiding a deeper issue. So try to check off the most important or difficult item first.

Most successful people have rituals they go through in the morning and at various points during the day that anchor them in what matters most and allow for the proper balance between exertion and recovery, which is necessary for achieving optimum performance throughout the day and throughout your life. Staying anchored is even more vital when you're emergineering your life, because your ability to be congruent with your highest vision and live in that vibration—the key to engineering your Emergence—has everything to do with what you're focused on moment by moment throughout the day. While time management and prioritization are important, *energy* management is even more so.

A ritual to support energy management might include waking up at a certain time, drinking a big glass of water, doing some exercise or yoga, meditating, praying, or reading inspiring material and then eating a healthy, nourishing meal. Then every 90 to 120 minutes you could take a stretch break, get another glass of water or a protein snack, take a short walk, or meditate—doing one of your Daily LIFT practices—to allow for recovery before jumping back in. If you start to incorporate these practices into your day, you'll find you're more alert, more focused, and more productive—and don't experience a late-afternoon crash. No matter what line of work or situation you find yourself in, the principle is always the same: don't let your life be the effect of external circumstances—rather, *be the cause* of your life.

Take some time now to design your greatest day. Include all you want and must accomplish to feel a sense of completion when you lay your head down at night. Remember to include all the life structures that matter—your inner and outer work, your personal and professional outcomes. After you complete this, you may want to revisit your weekly plan and see if it needs to be adjusted.

Sticking with a success ritual won't always be easy, but as you practice, it'll strengthen your ability to be present and focused on what matters most, which will have a transferring effect on your inner work. Remember, Emergence is not some quick-fix tool or technique; it's a way of life. To become a master of it—in fact, to become a master of anything—we must embrace everything in our life as part of our path. As Pelé, one of the greatest soccer players and overall athletes in history, said, "Everything is practice."[2]

Living in Your Zone of Genius

As we've been discussing, creating a powerful, structurally sound plan and following a success ritual that incorporates your Daily LIFT practices are all in service to becoming more of who you really are— that is, in service to your Emergence. Organizing your life around these structures allows you to begin living more from your "zone of genius"—that talent or set of skills that is uniquely part of your soul's purpose—giving more time and attention to what's authentically yours to be and do, until that's all you do. One motto I've endeavored to live by for years is, "Delegate everything but your brilliance."[3] It's how nature is structured.

Everything in nature has its unique purpose and function, and it does only or mostly that, leaving everything else to the rest of nature. This ultimately creates an intricate yet efficient ecosystem. If nature's flora and fauna tried to live the way humans do, where the oak tree was also trying to do a little pine-tree work on the side and the bee was moonlighting as a hummingbird, things would quickly fall apart. We don't see this as clearly in human experience. We've taken for granted that this is just the way things are, but we have some examples of what's possible when people structure their lives around their zone of genius.

It looks like the birth of Western thought, with figures like Plato and Aristotle, who devoted their days to their singular passions of philosophical thought, discourse, and writing, or the Renaissance that gave rise to the brilliant artist and inventor da Vinci and the uniquely gifted sculptor Michelangelo. It looks like the genius composer Mozart, champion golfer Tiger Woods, and the Polgár sisters, the greatest chess trio in history, all of whom were the products not of chance, luck, or some divine dispensation but of a methodically crafted vision, structure, and plan to focus on and live in their zone of genius from the day they could walk (or sooner).

We now know that success, genius, and accomplishment at the highest level are not the result of some special grace or talent granted only to the lucky few but of focused activity toward a singular pursuit, in a structure that removes most of the other activities that distract us—in other words, a clear vision, plan, and daily practice. So organize your life around those areas or activities where you bring the most value, feel the most strength, and create the most consistent results. Then find the people, systems, and support structures to do the rest. As you master the art of quantum planning, it might mean hiring someone to mow your lawn, clean your house, or do your accounting, taxes, and other things that someone else can do just as well or better. It's okay if you can't delegate every extraneous task now, but begin thinking this way. It's easier to design this into your life before you have a lot of momentum. When you've already got all the balls and plates and chainsaws in the air, it's much more difficult to reorganize and delegate without sending things crashing down around you.

Take some time now to consider what kind of support you might need, what possible systems you could engineer into your life, and thus your plan, from the beginning. One of your goals might include "find a great assistant, gardener, or bookkeeper." Be creative. If you don't have the budget to pay for the extra help, maybe you can barter something. Maybe you can find an intern who would see assisting you in your work as a valuable learning experience or could get college credit for it. There's always a way. At the very least, include a plan to get support so that you're focusing your energy where you should: on your one- and five-year visions.

The Plan to Plan

One of the greatest ironies is that we're often so busy living the lives we don't want that we can't find time to plan the life we do. We want more time, and we can see that a plan could give us that, but we don't have time to create more time! Don't let the experience of "no time" prevent you from taking the time to create your plan. Don't let this drag on for weeks and months or you'll lose momentum. I know you're busy—we all are—but I also know from firsthand experience that that's often just an excuse that keeps us from moving forward.

If your life depended on your creating a plan in the next thirty days, would you say, "Gosh, I just don't have time"? I realize that's pretty dramatic, but in a very real way, your life *does* depend on it; you just might not see it now. That's how the ego keeps us static; we don't realize the importance of something until we look back on it. So rather than waiting for your own hindsight, I invite you to lean on mine. After working with people for two decades, watching them postpone their plan until they lost momentum, I have the benefit of a *lot* of hindsight. I know what happens for most people at this point, and my intention is that you don't become a statistic—that this process doesn't become more "shelf help." The truth is that many, if not all, of the things you think are holding you back aren't. They have no power at all. You're more resourceful, capable, innovative, and brilliant than you can imagine. By the time you finish, you'll be more acquainted with that version of yourself.

I propose a challenge: plan a block of time over the next two weeks and commit to working this out, at least enough to get you in motion. That might mean blocking out a few hours each weekend or even longer. It might mean scheduling a few hours during the week and/or some time each day. It might mean sitting down with your loved ones and explaining that you're focusing on this for the next couple of weeks and might not be as available. In other words, you'll need to create a supportive structure—*a plan to plan*—in order to create a plan for fulfilling your highest vision. But is there anything more important? If you don't know where you're going, every road will take you there. If you're not living *your* plan, you're living someone else's. And if you're not living the life you were born for, you're not really living your life at all.

Life doesn't hold anything back from us; we hold ourselves back from life. So do whatever it takes to get this done, even if you're used to thinking that it's not possible. When you look back on this moment, you'll be able to say, *That was the moment that changed everything.* Like those students who created their own paths out of the chaotic landscape of their campus, you'll see that the desire path you were waiting to appear is being carved by *you*, moment by moment, day by day, guided by an inner design that is leading you back to yourself—where all the riches you've been waiting for have been waiting for you all along.

STAGE FOUR

GIVE WHAT
APPEARS MISSING

You only keep what you give away.

SHELDON KOPP

"My husband and I can't say two words to each other without drawing blood," Jill cried to her therapist. "The second he walks through the door, we're at each other's throats. Deep down, I know the love's still there, but it seems hopelessly buried."

Listening intently, the therapist reached into his drawer, pulled out a bottle, and handed it to her. "This is holy water, blessed by a swami from India," he said. "For the next week, whenever your husband's about to enter the room, take a drink, hold some on your tongue, and look into his eyes. After a couple of seconds, swallow it. You should notice an improvement in your interactions right away."

Jill went home and waited eagerly for her other half to return. When he walked in, she took a swig of the blessed water and silently held his gaze. He gave her a suspicious look, and then grinned curiously. She swallowed the water and asked how his day had gone. Amazingly, they didn't argue. In fact, they had one of their most intimate talks in recent memory. The next night before he came to bed, Jill snuck another jolt of the powerful liquid, performing the same ritual. After a few moments, it was as if a veil were lifted and she saw him in a whole new light, saw him for the first time again . . . saw the man she had fallen in love with. The predictable fight never came. And the rest of the night was anything but predictable.

The following week, with her water supply depleted and her love life nearly replenished, Jill returned to the therapist, proclaiming that the treatment was healing her marriage and that she needed to get ahold of more holy water . . . fast.

The therapist smiled and revealed that the "magical potion" was nothing but store-bought Mountain Spring bottled water. The power that healed her relationship wasn't from some swami in India or some sacred elixir; it had been in her all along.

You Are the Answer You've Been Seeking

So what created this outcome for Jill? Was it her expectation or intention or the result of breaking a habit? Certainly these are important. But something else was going on here. In choosing silence over her conditioned response, she pressed the pause button on the inner movie projector that had been replaying old conflicts. And in that space, she made room for something new, something more authentic and loving—her deeper nature—to emerge. She also created the conditions for her partner to do the same.

She momentarily stepped out of the story that her partner was the problem and that it was something *he* wasn't giving that was missing, and allowed something more to come out of *her*. Instead of waiting for him to listen, she listened to him; instead of waiting for him to see her, she looked long enough to really see him; instead of blaming and remaining a victim of her circumstance, she took back the power and showed up to the relationship in a way she wanted him to. It may have been mostly "accidental," but an important principle was nevertheless revealed:

Everything she thought was missing from the relationship had been in her all along, just waiting for her to become congruent with it and let it out.

We have been conditioned to believe that if something seems lacking, we have to go out and get it or cajole, control, and complain until someone gives it to us. But the opposite is true: we must find what appears missing within *ourselves* and let it out.

Living according to the false notion that we have to go outside ourselves to get what we want has led to the majority of our lack, limitation, greed, and conflict. But in this stage, you'll learn how to turn that around by understanding that whatever's missing is what *you're* not giving. The Universal Mind, the Kingdom of Heaven, Nirvana—they are all within you. The way to experience it, however, is not by dying and going there but by living—and giving—*from* there.

This applies to everything that appears missing in your life. If you want more respect, respect others more; if you want more love, love more fully; if you want an ideal partner, *become* an ideal partner by radiating the qualities you're seeking. In this chapter you'll be guided to identify key areas where you feel you've become stuck, waiting for some person or condition to change, and learn strategies to start giving what you've been trying to get—first to yourself and then to the people and environments where the lack appears. This reverses the flow of energy, making you the *cause* in your world instead of feeling like you're at the effect of it, empowering you to generate whatever raw materials your vision requires.

The importance of this stage can't be overstated: when you realize that *everything* you need is within you—not metaphorically but literally—the whole meaning and purpose of your life changes. You are set free from the shackles of economic, social, and governmental dependence that enslaves most people, and you become the leaven that lifts everyone around you.

The Great Reversal

We've been taught that life happens *to* us and that we must find better ways to deflect, dodge, or dance with it in order to get what we want and get rid of what we don't. While mastering these coping mechanisms may have helped us survive as a species, we've evolved to a place where they're now limiting our evolution. Just as the seed already contains the pattern for the plant and the soil it's planted in contains the nutrients for its growth, the seed planted in the soil of our soul contains everything we need to grow. So actualizing our greater potential is not a process of coping, defending, or fighting our way to the next level; it's a process of activating this inherent potential.

As individualized expressions of divine love and intelligence, we didn't come here to get anything but, rather, to release this imprisoned splendor. We really are God's gift to the world. Living otherwise—striving to get from the world—sets up a belief of lack that you will continuously experience and blocks the emergence of the gifts you came here to give. Played out to its extreme, this false premise leads to all the horrible acts of corruption and violence. We're willing to lie, cheat, and steal for something *that is already within us.* We diminish or destroy countless relationships because they don't give us the love, respect, and validation *that only we can activate within ourselves.* And we are willing to hurt, betray, or kill our neighbor—including our neighbors across the oceans—to get *that which they can never give us.* In the West, we have more abundance than at any time in history, yet we are some of the unhappiest people on the planet. You can never get enough of what you don't really need. In fact, you can never feed that insatiable hunger by "getting" anything. Because you already have everything, it's only through giving that you can experience having. Only through letting the light within shine can your own life be illuminated.

Through Emergence, giving *is* receiving.

The great reversal is not only realizing that everything we need is within us but also realizing that everything we need is spiritual.

The reason we're so attached to material things and why we think that someone or something out there has our happiness is because we have materialized the spirit instead of spiritualizing the material. What we come to realize as we do this work is that no amount of material things can bring real peace or fulfillment. However, when we connect with and release our inner spirit, it can take the *forms* of external fulfillment. The fruit tree illustrates this. A farmer doesn't hoard the crop, fearing that if he gives it away he'll never have any more. He understands that the fruit is the *effect* of an invisible cause within the tree; it is a symbol of the real wealth of the tree, which is the invisible process that allows the roots to turn the raw soil into sap, blossom, and fruit. So when, in winter, the tree is bare, the farmer doesn't lose faith and cut it down, because he knows the tree is just as abundant as ever.

Likewise, even when the landscape of your life (or bank account) seems barren, you're still infinitely rich because it is the invisible process within you, a process that turns the soil of your soul into the thoughts, actions, and forms of your world that constitutes your real wealth and worth. The world can never add to this or take it away; it can only reflect what you are allowing to emerge. As long as you remain rooted in your soul and cultivate the inner conditions that are congruent with the seed of your potential, you will produce a bountiful harvest season after season.

You Can Only Give What You Have

While it's true that you already have all you need within, you can't experience this reality by merely knowing it intellectually. To "have" something, you must *consciously* participate in it. Earlier we discussed moving from anticipation of future good to participating in the good already here, within and around us. This activates it in consciousness, making it "real," giving you the actual experience of *having* it. A mistake many heart-centered or spiritual seekers make is trying to give what they don't have—what hasn't been activated in consciousness. The result is often stress, self-doubt, stagnation, resentment, feeling burned out or broke from all their giving, and even sometimes making things worse for those they're trying to help. (There's nothing worse than a resentful giver!)

It's simple to understand: If you don't breathe in, you can't breathe out. If you don't receive, you won't have anything to give. It's one constant flow, in and out, back and forth, with no beginning or end. You don't take in a breath and hold it; it must be released. Similarly, we don't hold on to the gifts we have, be they material or spiritual. We receive, share what we have, and receive again. This is the Law of Circulation.

Receiving is not the same as "getting," however. When you're trying to get something, you're often forcing, pushing, and coming from a place of fear, lack, or limitation. But when you allow yourself to receive what's coming to you—whether it's your next breath, a loving gesture, money, or any of the riches all around—it's a gracious act of allowing that requires no effort. What's more, it allows for the cycle of life and the circulation of energy to find completion—as well as a new beginning—in you.

One of the most generous things you can do for another is to allow them to give to you. Think about acts of love you've given to another—a compliment, a gift, or some compensation for a job well done. Didn't it feel great to be able to give it to them? Now think of a time when you tried to give that word of praise, gift, or act of kindness and it wasn't graciously accepted. How did that feel? When someone doesn't allow the energy to circulate *to* them, the cycle is incomplete and it can feel stuck. God is always trying to pour through you, around you, and to you—even when it comes through others. It's one circulation, one flow; it's the way Infinite Wholeness manifests. And the more you say yes to this circulation, the more you'll receive and the more you'll have to give in an endless upward spiral of abundance.

Of course, life doesn't always appear to be so generous to us. When this happens, it's not personal. The universe is just reflecting how we're thinking about or treating *ourselves*, such as "undeserving" or "not good enough." But we can change this flow by actively giving to ourselves. This can be hard for heart-centered people. If the idea of receiving feels selfish, the idea of actively *giving to ourselves* and meeting all our needs may feel almost blasphemous. It can bring up guilt and shame because somewhere we got the message that it's wrong to take care of ourselves and we've found validation in taking care of others. But the truth is that to *not* fill yourself up (to not breathe in) and meet your needs first is simply futile. Like the familiar analogy of the oxygen mask in an airplane: when the pressure drops and the masks fall, if you try to help others before putting on your own mask first, you'll pass out and be of no use to anyone else.

Only when you participate in the abundance all around you can you be truly generous. Only when you *have* can you *give*. Only when you've taken care of your needs can you truly take care of another in the deepest sense. Anything else is a manipulative trick of the ego, acting like it's giving in order to obtain a feeling of worth, validation, or approval.

Remember, the nature of abundance and fulfillment is not a static thing; it's a constant flow of breathing in, breathing out, giving and receiving. It's important that you give, serve, or share with others, even while you're accepting what is given and allowing yourself to be served. From the Emergence paradigm, giving is receiving and receiving is giving; taking care of yourself is taking care of others, and taking care of others is taking care of yourself. It's all one action, one breath—and, spiritually, it all carries the same energy.

Let's expand our spiritual lung capacity.

Improving Your Circulation

Think about one area of your life where you feel stuck, at the effect of another person or situation, unable to move forward or get what you need. What are you waiting to see, hear, or receive before you can feel empowered? Maybe it's an intimate partner you've been waiting to get respect or validation from. Perhaps it's a boss who hasn't given you the approval you feel you deserve. It might be a financial situation, where you believe that you can't move forward until you have a certain amount of money or a physical issue that has convinced you that it's impossible to move in the direction of your dreams.

Ask yourself what qualities you would need to embody in order to be free and fulfilled in this situation, even if the condition didn't change. For example, if the situation concerning you is a seeming lack of money, maybe the quality you'd need to embody would be a sense of security, a feeling that all is well. If it's a relationship where you're not being validated, maybe it would be feeling good about yourself. Write these qualities down.

Next, look at this situation again and ask, "What does this thing I want/need/lack represent to me? What does it stand for or symbolize?" This is another way to look for clues into the deeper meaning of what is missing. For example, let's say it's a job you're wanting. You might discover that it stands for safety, power, or a sense of feeling useful. Write down any symbolic meanings you associate with having a job.

Visualize yourself getting that ideal job you've been waiting for. Let yourself *feel* it. At your own pace, breathe and let this feeling expand, filling your chest and then your whole body. If you can sense even a glimmer of the quality that would make you feel fulfilled, you've demonstrated the key to your freedom: *that your ability to experience this quality has nothing to do with anyone or anything outside of you.* If money, rather than a job, was the area where you felt stuck and you're now experiencing a feeling of abundance or security (or whatever qualities you listed), you have just proven that money—this outside object—is not, and never was, the cause of any feelings of abundance or security you've been yearning for.

It doesn't matter how slight the feeling is. With practice it will grow stronger until it's a luminous glow within. This practice builds the Soul Purpose Pillar of *feeling*. And as this feeling integrates, that new vibration or consciousness will dissolve the fear and sense of lack that has been holding you back and become the very substance of the next stage of your Emergence (the same way the soil becomes the sap, blossom, and fruit). You, and you alone, are at the controls of this process. You are not at the effect of your conditions; you are the cause.

Now ask yourself, "Who would I *be* if this situation were resolved fully? How would I hold myself? How would I act?" This expands your awareness to include the Soul Purpose Pillar of *being*. Write down these qualities of being. And, again, take a moment to really experience what it's like to *be* this person who fully embodies the qualities you've described. As you do, you're activating that state of being, and over time, it will begin to integrate in your consciousness as a new vibratory set point. But there's more you can do to anchor these qualities in your mind, body, and experience.

Look at the qualities of being and ask, "What would it look like to be this person in my life now?" Don't accept a vague answer like "be more authentic." Ask what specifically that would look like. Ask until you get actionable guidance. For example, "Be more authentic" may lead to, "Tell my spouse how I am really feeling about his working late," or, "Tell my boss what my real vision is for this project." Finally, ask, "What activities, people, environments, or objects make me *feel* the way I would feel if this situation were resolved?" (This should be familiar from your earlier work with the Soul Purpose Pillars in Stage Two.) Make a list of the possibilities. Integrate the ones that resonate the most with you into your quantum plan.

To accelerate your Emergence in this area, create a focused weekly strategy that includes

- At least one way you can be the person you would be if this situation were resolved.

- One to three activities that make you feel these feelings of empowerment.

- Some quality time with people who make you feel these feelings.

- At least one trip to an environment that makes you feel these feelings.

- One to three objects (pictures, music, scents, trinkets) that activate these feelings.

Working these elements into your calendar will help you avoid falling back into habitual activities that are not congruent with the higher frequencies of what you desire. After the first week, reevaluate whether you've chosen the right people, places, and things to support your Emergence. If the situation requires more work, create a longer-term strategy.

You Can Only Keep What You Give

Now that you're starting to activate a greater feeling of having, the next piece is to radiate it into your experience by giving it away. This isn't some metaphysical trick. You're not giving to get, which brings you back to the old paradigm of lacking something. As we've already discussed, you're giving because *giving is the mechanism by which we bring what is needed into our world.*

Nothing enters this world except through the act of giving or expressing. And the act of giving something from the consciousness of *having* allows you to lock that new frequency into place, like a preset button on your radio. Both are necessary. The more you give *from an awareness of having*, the more you have to give. We understand this principle as it applies to knowledge; the more a teacher teaches, the more knowledge she gains. It's the act of sharing her knowledge with her students (giving) that increases, activates, and magnifies it without limit. We see it also with qualities like courage or gratitude. The more we express them, the more of them we have; our depth of feeling and understanding grows.

When it comes to other aspects of life, however, we often enter a thicket of negative beliefs. If our heart has been broken, we might hoard our love like a scarce resource and end up experiencing less love—not because there isn't enough love coming to us but because we're not allowing more love to come *through* us. Likewise, we might withhold support, respect, validation, or approval because we don't feel we're getting enough of it ourselves, believing that if we hold on to it, someone will eventually give it to us. It never works. We might fear that if we give the praise and validation we ourselves feel lacking, we'll so empower others that they won't need us anymore. But where does this end? With both parties feeling *less* supported, respected, or validated, not only does the good stop expanding but it atrophies like an unused muscle. As it says in Matthew 13:12, "To the one who has, more will be given, and he will have an abundance, but from the one who has not, even what he has will be taken away."

This also goes for material things, like charitable contributions. If we feel lacking in money, it's a true test of faith to give some of the little we have. It's not the amount but the intention. Giving should feel like a stretch but not so much that you pull a muscle. As you give from a place of feeling abundant, it accelerates the Law of Circulation in your life, and the universe, which is always seeking to fulfill itself through you, now sees you as a willing and able channel through which it can pour Itself.

Other challenging types of giving include supporting someone who isn't supporting us, helping others become successful when we want others to help us, or being a friend and companion when we're feeling desperate for love and affection ourselves. The more we're willing to help others achieve what we want, treat others how we want to be treated, and support others in the way we want support—not giving to get but expressing, from a consciousness of having, what is needed in the world—the more we activate and expand those qualities within ourselves. These qualities then radiate into our environment and become the people, places, and opportunities that form the next stage of our evolution.

As you begin to radiate or give these seemingly missing qualities, *don't forget to include yourself.* As discussed above, this is often a soul lesson for heart-centered people or those from a background where hard work and self-sacrifice is a core value. But it's essential that you practice this self-care, whatever your background or beliefs. Don't just activate these within you—actively give them to yourself.

As you do this, some interesting things can happen. Not only will you have a greater sense of these qualities yourself but you will also become free of the illusion that anyone or anything was ever your source of fulfillment. The ego will fight to pull you back with self-talk like, "How can you keep loving, respecting, and validating this person when they're not giving these things to you?" and "How can you keep giving your all to this job when it's not what you're meant to do? Besides, nobody even appreciates you." But if you're willing to stay the course, you'll not only overcome that self-talk but you'll also keep growing as if you *are* in your ideal situation or relationship and become the person you would be if you *were* loved, appreciated, approved of, and validated!

At this stage, one of two things happens: If the other person or situation is willing and able to match you at this higher frequency, things will improve and expand, often in ways you can't imagine. And if a match isn't possible, the universe will move you into an environment or relationship that *can* interact with you at this new level. Just be aware that the new situation may not appear immediately. There is often a period of settling, deeper integration, and what feels like a final test of the new boundaries—like your soul saying, "Are you sure you're up to this?"—before the manifestation takes place. This can also happen while you're in the old experience, as was the case with the following story. But take heart. When the shift happens, because consciousness always precedes form, the outer reality *must* conform to your new level of being.

How I Learned to Stop Waiting and Start Serving

After my initial spiritual opening and the period of deeper work that followed for several years, I ended up out of work, with little cash flow. Where the path of many actors is to go from being a waiter to a working performer, I did it in reverse: I went from being an up-and-coming actor to a down-and-out waiter, waiting on people I had been in movies with. It was a humbling experience, to put it mildly. While I didn't have my pride anymore, I did have a vision: I wanted to use my creative talents to inspire and transform people. And although I didn't have any prospects for making that happen, I had the basic tools of Emergence to make it welcome (although I didn't have the language for it then). So I began to practice this principle of giving what appears missing by showing up every day to my waiter role as if it were my dream job, intending to be the person I believed I would be if I were living my destiny.

I began to bring a level of excellence, giving five-star service in a three-star restaurant. I stopped complaining and joining with the other waiters in criticizing customers. I focused on being grateful, having fun, activating joy and passion, and holding everyone I came in contact with in the highest regard. Step by step, I expressed more of the qualities of character that were congruent with my higher vision and let go of behaviors that weren't. Customers started giving me high praise and higher tips, saying they would contact the corporate office to say they'd received the best service they'd ever had.

My star was finally shining.

So the manager fired me.

I don't remember why. Something about "not being a good fit." But after a brief period of discussion—and the support of another manager who pointed out that I hadn't actually done anything wrong—they hired me back. I felt misunderstood, mistreated, and somewhat of a pariah, but I took it as a challenge and dug deeper, activating the qualities of my vision, generating the qualities of my higher character, cleaning up my judgment about the staff, reaching out to help and serve even more. And pretty soon I was humming again, feeling even better, more empowered than ever.

So they fired me again.

This time something had actually happened, something they could point to. *It just didn't have anything to do with me.* And after a period of investigation, they discovered it was a mistake. Someone had scapegoated me or made an error. And they hired me back.

The staff started regarding me with sideways glances and some decided I was up to no good. I felt alienated, alone, and basically a loser. But I needed this job (although the feeling of need was dissolving). So I dug deeper. I asked, "Where else am I not acting with integrity?" And began to find places where I was feeling inadequate, looking for approval and validation, and being dishonest. For example, I started to suspect that the rolls and sodas I was helping myself to in the back was stealing. I had told myself that everyone else was doing it, and it seemed like the norm. But increasingly, I couldn't help wondering why we were all sneaky about it. And when I asked myself why I didn't just pay for them, I discovered a pocket of poverty consciousness—a part of me that, on some level, felt like I had to lie or cheat to get what I wanted and needed. I didn't want to lose my free rolls and sodas, but I was too aware of this inner breach of integrity, so I mustered up the courage to ask the manager if it was okay. As expected, she said no.

Bit by bit, I cleaned up these little lies and cheats, becoming more congruent in my inner and outer life. While it was difficult to let go of these comforts and conveniences I had become accustomed to, I started feeling good again, more empowered, even inspired to do my job. I looked for more ways to extend my service, to bring more value to the customers and the staff. This time I was certain I had clicked. I had finally arrived.

So, of course, they fired me again!

I decided to stay fired this time. I figured the universe was definitely sending me a message. The great thing was that I didn't have any grudges; I didn't blame them. I felt like it was all in divine order. My fiancée, on the other hand, wanted to torch the place. When I would

suggest we eat there, she'd be beside herself, wondering how I could
ever consider going there again. I understood—and appreciated—her
feelings. She was just standing by her man. But inside me, there was
no animosity. I was free. And within a short time, I was hired to perform and teach communication and interpersonal skills to the top
executives of Fortune 500 companies. I went from waiting on tables
in a three-star restaurant to being wined and dined in five-star restaurants around the country, making twenty times what I made as
a waiter.

As I lifted my vibration on that waiter's job, that environment
couldn't rise to match me. That's not a judgment; it's just the nature
of the situation. Besides, it wasn't *meant* to match me. As we grow up,
we don't wear the same size shoes or pants. We even outgrow people,
places, and life purposes. (You can't actually outgrow your purpose,
but you can and must outgrow your limited perception of it.) That
doesn't make the different sizes and shapes wrong. You don't have
to make someone or something wrong to move on; you just need to
know that it doesn't fit *you* anymore.

Another key takeaway from this experience is that the bigger
life and opportunity didn't happen in my future; it happened in that
waiter's job. We create the mental-emotional equivalent of the larger
life we desire while exercising our potential in the smaller, seemingly limited experience. The boundaries and limitations act as an
inner gymnasium for our soul, which uses all that resistance to get
stronger. If we wait for a better opportunity to come along, instead
of embracing the one in front of us and showing up as the person we
envision we can be, we won't develop the consciousness congruent
with that larger life. And should we somehow still manage to manifest it, we will struggle to maintain it. We've seen this with some
who experience overnight success or come into a sudden financial
windfall, like the lottery winner who ends up broke all over again or
in debt worse than before.

The phases of Emergence are illustrated by a baby chick in an egg. At a certain point, the chick uses up its resources, pollutes its environment, and becomes too big for its shell. It's cramped and hungry, and the place stinks. If it had self-consciousness, it might feel like a victim, believing that life was against it, God was against it, that it was a sinner being punished, or that everything was its parents' fault for abandoning it to these terrible conditions. However, if through prayer, affirmations, or a do-gooding farmer, it were freed from its shell, it would die.

Fortunately, the chick is governed by nature's laws and instead starts pecking and scratching, looking for any source of good in its environment. It doesn't bemoan what it *can't* do; it does what it *can*. It doesn't focus on what's *missing*; it focuses on any morsel of good it has, utilizing all its abilities and resources to maximum capacity. As it does, the pecking not only cracks the egg and frees the chick but also strengthens its neck muscles and lungs, readying it to thrive in the larger world.

Unstuck for Life

One of the powerful realizations gleaned from these examples is that you never have to remain a victim of circumstance, and despite appearances, you're never really stuck. Will you have challenges? Yes. Will you feel backed into a corner with no seeming solution? Most likely. Will outer conditions continue to change? Change is the nature of human experience. But none of this can make you a victim or keep you victimized when you've suffered a setback if you embrace the truth that you are a divine power plant. You don't need to wait for energy or go out and get it when you can generate it yourself. No matter what conditions you're faced with, you can activate and radiate whatever you need into your inner and outer environment and begin the process of renewal and Emergence.

None of this is to suggest that we condone people or actions that hurt us or others. Holding abusers accountable for their misdeeds is a part of the healing process. This also doesn't take away your right to feel all your feelings and care for the wounded places within. An all-embracing self-love is fundamental to healing—and to the Emergence model, as you'll see in Stage Six. As stated earlier, this is not about "blaming the victim." It's about becoming free and living in your full power. Understandably, this is not always easy, especially if you've experienced real trauma at the hands of another. But in nearly every case where a victim of abuse has recovered, some version of this process has been part of their path back to wholeness.

So I invite you to consider what your life would be like if you knew you could never be a victim again—or at the very least, knew you could never be kept in a state of victimization. How would you hold yourself? Would your back be a little straighter, your head held a little higher? Would you have a bit more spring in your step? Would you take more risks, stand up, and stand out—even a little more? Would you lower your guard, take down the walls, open your heart, and stretch out your hand? Feel into that. Imagine the possibilities. Find that place of willingness within you to embrace this principle and set yourself free.

But the end of victimhood is just the beginning of your new level of power. What if you could never be stuck again?

For many, being stuck seems a chronic state. But as we do this work, the truth becomes clear: being stuck is a *belief*, an issue of perspective. It only has power over us when we stay focused on our stuck-ness instead of on where we desire to go. No matter what your situation is, there's always something you can do to keep moving, to change channels—mentally, emotionally, spiritually, or physically. And once you get moving in one dimension of your being, you begin freeing up others.

For example, if you believe you're stuck in a relationship, you can imagine the kind of relationship you *want* to be in and then feel what it would feel like. This will immediately get your energy moving again. From there, you can notice who you would *be* if you were in that ideal relationship and ask, "How can I step into being this person more fully *now*?" This will give you guidance, direction, and your next action—and just like that, you're not stuck anymore. No matter how dire the situation, no matter what appears lacking, missing, or making you feel stuck, if you apply the principle that "whatever's missing is what you're not giving" and follow the practices in this chapter, you'll *immediately start moving again*—moving your energy higher, expanding your state of *being* in your environment, or getting guidance on your next steps. It's always seeking to emerge, ready to express, when you align with and allow it.

Imagine never feeling trapped, stalled, repressed, or held back. Excuses fly out the window. Procrastination becomes impossible. What would your life look like if this were true? Would you wake up with more joy in your heart and excitement for your day? Would you be willing to start that project you've been putting off? Would you glide through life with more grace and power? Take some time now to contemplate this, to journal about it. The stronger you feel the possibilities with this principle, the more motivated you'll be to apply it.

The Thirty-Day Giving Challenge

The biblical statement "Ask and you will receive"(John 16:24) might more accurately be stated, "Give and you will receive." Although I've already discussed the importance of giving as a means of circulating more of your inner spiritual substance or life force, it's so crucial to the understanding and activation of Emergence that it deserves the final word. Put simply,

Giving is the most powerful method for getting all we want in life.

Not in a cynical way. Giving should not be used as manipulation to get something. If you're giving to get, you're out of alignment with this truth. But as you understand this principle, you'll see that the whole universe is within. There's nothing more to get "out there"; there's just more inside trying to get out. When you live from that place, it'll look like you're getting more, but you're really just letting more emerge.

Consider, from this day forward, being all about giving, asking every morning, "How can I be a bigger giver?" Then look for ways to give—to yourself, your loved ones, your colleagues, and the world. I invite you to commit to doing this every day for the next thirty days and watch what emerges. As you turn on that divine power plant within, there's nothing you won't be able to accomplish according to your soul's plan. You can even create a specific Thirty-Day Giving Challenge, where you identify all the places you've been withholding, waiting, and trying to get, and then write down all the ways you can be a bigger giver—all the places in your life that you can start generating, radiating, and pouring forth your untapped potential. Use this list to become a bigger giver each day, even in the smallest of ways.

Think of how powerful the sun must feel being able to shine in all its fullness with no agenda. That's what you're capable of— walking through this world, so tuned in and turned on, ablaze with the light of the divine, seeking nothing and giving everything. You'll become unstoppable. More than that, you'll be a blessing to everyone who crosses your path. The universe will flow through you, to you, and around you—all the heavenly riches you could ever imagine and beyond.

This is the great promise of all masters through the ages.

You are the light of the world.

So power up, and let it shine.

STAGE FIVE

ACT AS IF YOU'RE IT

To him who can perfectly practice inaction,
all things are possible.

ERNEST HOLMES

Dressed in my desert-sand army camouflage, I sat in one of the more romantic booths at Ernie's tacos, staring at a dusty oil painting of a matador facing off the snorting beast he was about to conquer. It was an unimpressive mechanical rendering, but something about it touched me. He was fearless, he knew his place, and the look in his eyes said that nothing would stop him from doing what was in his true nature.

I'm referring to the bull.

I didn't care about the matador. He had all the odds in his favor. He had a sword, a cheering crowd, and a trapped animal—it was all a show. But the bull . . . the bull wasn't there for a show. He didn't ask to be there. He was there because he had to be. He was there by some act of fate. There was something about him that was so true, so authentic. He was an expression of pure intention. I wanted that bull to win. He *deserved* to win. I don't know; maybe it was the margarita talking.

As I licked the salt off a still-warm tortilla chip, dipped it into Ernie's famous chunky herb salsa, and took a bite, savoring the tang, I nervously contemplated what was about to happen. Not to the bull, but to me. I had just returned from the Persian Gulf conflict, and any minute my fiancée would be arriving. It would be the first time I'd seen her since I deployed. She was the one thing that had kept me going, the first thought on my mind when I awoke at 5:00 AM in that dusty hell, the last thought on my mind when I stared up at the warm Arabian night before drifting off to sleep. I was so in love with her, I could barely stand it.

Unfortunately, none of it was real.

I wasn't a soldier. And she wasn't my fiancée. She wasn't even my girlfriend.

Okay, let me back up. You see, I was an actor, and this rendezvous at Ernie's was an acting exercise that my partner, Elizabeth, and I had devised in order to practice living under an imaginary situation outside of class. The idea was that if we could fool everyone around us and really *believe it ourselves*, we would be better actors for it. It was my idea to have the whole romantic angle. The truth is, I was kind of into her. All right, I was *totally* into her. But she wasn't available, so . . . if I couldn't actually be with her, then at least I could *act* like I was for a few precious moments. I even wrote a love letter (as if from the Persian Gulf) where I confessed that she was the only thing that kept me alive during those endless days and brutal conflicts. Then I had it delivered to her.

Sitting there waiting for her, slightly buzzed from the tequila— or maybe the intense smell of burning grease—I was really getting into my part.

When Elizabeth arrived, we were already in character. We embraced like long-lost lovers, professed how much we missed each other, and cried. Real tears. (Hey, this was method acting; we *never* faked it.) She slid in beside me, our hands clenched tightly together, and we began to catch up. I had prepared well, so I had lots to tell her, including the tragic loss of my best friend, who had died in my arms. We both cried some more. Then she shared her news: she was pregnant. We were going to have a baby! We embraced, shed more tears, laughed at the craziness of it all, waxed about fate and destiny . . . and then kissed. *Really kissed.*

Method actors and all.

And that's when I realized something strange had happened.

At some point in all the laughing and crying and the talk about death and birth, fate and destiny, it stopped being an act . . . and I was in love for real. I say "was" in love instead of "fell" in love because it didn't feel like it was just beginning; it felt like tuning in to a broadcast already in progress.

I took hold of her and kissed her, wiping the tears from her eyes, then mine, and then kissed her again. But this time it was a little *too* real for her. She gently pulled away, looked at her watch, and told me she had to get to work but that she would be home later tonight and we would continue to catch up; she wanted to hear everything. We hugged, and I slipped in another kiss before she slipped out of the booth and was gone. She didn't even look back.

That should have ended it, right? I should have taken my cue, paid the bill, called an available girl, and had a real date. Instead, I returned home and proceeded to wait for her. And wait. Until I couldn't wait any longer and called the place she said she worked at. I had to hear her voice again.

They told me she didn't work there. Never did.

What? Why would she lie to me? The woman I loved!

I called my best friend and asked him to keep me company. I was confused and basically freaking out. I didn't know what to believe now. The line between fiction and reality had completely blurred. Was she coming over after all? Or was that parting promise just her final line of dialogue as she made a hasty exit stage right? I knew that what I felt in that booth was real. And I was pretty sure she had felt it too. *This was not a fantasy*, I told myself. She *was* coming over at ten that night. I had to have faith in what I felt.

I paced back and forth for more than an hour, trying to talk things through with my friend, watching the clock tick down the minutes to 10:00 PM . . . then 10:15, 10:30. Maybe she was just running late, had a last-minute rush. That happens at restaurants all the time, right? *What the hell was I thinking?* She didn't even work at that restaurant, maybe not at *any* restaurant. She was probably sitting at a bar somewhere, laughing to a friend about this weird guy from acting class who totally lost it in an exercise and started groping her like some total weirdo!

My friend finally had enough, told me to forget about her and get drunk, and then left. I was crushed. I literally fell into my bed like a teenage boy with a broken heart and scribbled out a (probably tear-stained) love poem on a piece of scratch paper:

The first thing on my mind when I awake, Elizabeth.
The last thing on my mind before I sleep, Elizabeth.
I'm sick with love and I don't want the cure.

Oh, yeah, it was *that* cheesy. I was not in a good place. I put it under my pillow, which I hugged as if it were her, and fell asleep.

But I couldn't let it go. For the next several weeks, I pursued her, asking her to help me rehearse auditions I had—auditions which, surprise, surprise, had kissing scenes. Like a good acting partner, she obliged, albeit somewhat suspiciously (and rightly so). And with every scene, that feeling I had experienced during our acting exercise came back.

I never got any of those parts we rehearsed.

But I got the girl.

About a year later, Elizabeth and I were engaged. About a year after that, we got married. Then had a baby. Then another. That was more than twenty years ago. And in the corner of our wedding picture is that silly little poem.

Action Is Belief in Work Clothes

Sometimes acting *as if* something is true activates something inside of us that really *is*. I had feelings for Elizabeth before that exercise, but it was the act of throwing myself into that imagined reality that flipped the switch within me and, eventually, for her as well. After that first "date," I had every reason to not pursue this. She didn't come after me; she didn't offer any clear sign of interest. But I had touched a reality inside myself, through the initial vision I'd created of our imagined relationship, the compelling backstory I'd prepared in advance, the inner work I'd done to generate a state of feeling and being in love, and finally the action of living as if it were so.

And it was my persistent action, from this state of feeling and *knowing* it was real, that finally made it so.

That experience was such a potent and practical demonstration to me that there was a principle at work that I began to think deeper about it. I began to wonder about all the times when I had wanted something and had done the inner work to believe I could have it but still hadn't achieved it. What I discovered was that, in many of those instances where I failed to fulfill my heart's desire, I hadn't fully invested in the new reality I was trying to create. I had affirmed and intended and even felt a level of inner conviction, but my consistent follow-through wasn't there. At some point, either because it got too hard, too scary, or brought up some unhealed wounds, my actions stopped being congruent with my deepest truth. My inner conviction and outer life were no longer in integrity; I was divided.

And divided, we fall.

This led me to begin asking myself a different set of questions. Questions based not on circumstances but on higher truth, universal principles. And when I honestly answered them and sincerely *acted* on those answers, it brought me back on track with my higher vision and allowed it to emerge in every area of my life.

I invite you to ask these questions for yourself in relation to the vision you're trying to bring forth:

• What would you *do* if you were totally loved and supported?

• What would you *do* if you were brilliant and talented?

• What would you *do* if you had everything you needed?

• What would you *do* if you knew you couldn't fail?

The answers to these questions and others I will be posing in this chapter lead to a new kind of action based on a fundamental affirmation of your being: that you are totally loved and supported, you *do* have everything you need, and you *are* inherently brilliant. The problem is, we've been hypnotized into believing we're something less than this, and many of our actions perpetuate that false premise. We believe we're lacking love or abundance, so we take actions to get or attract more, which exacerbates the consciousness of lack, even if we manage to muscle our way into more material goods. We believe we're unworthy or untalented, so we *don't* take action, which increases our sense of inadequacy, deepens our depression, and hobbles our abilities. Or we think that just "believing" is enough to make all our dreams come true and wait for something or someone to save us, rather than understanding that action isn't separate from believing. But action is the *evidence* of belief and the *mechanism* by which we anchor it on earth.

Action is belief in work clothes.

The main problem is twofold: We act or don't act based on a false identity or self-image (made up of false ideas we have about ourselves), bringing us out of integrity with our true nature. And when we do act—even if it's through metaphysical or other self-improvement techniques—we're trying to get something out there instead of realizing we need to let something within us out. As Robert Browning said, "Truth lies within ourselves: it takes no rise from outward things. There is an inmost center in us all, *where truth abides in fullness* and to Know rather consists in opening out a way whence the imprisoned splendor may escape."[1] Your deepest desires are clues of what's already in you, trying to come out. As you take action from this place of "already being the thing," your actions are not trying to achieve it; rather, they're an expression of alignment with it, *an affirmation of your true nature*. From that place, there's no more resistance, no more negation, and you become an opening through which the next stage of your greater Self becomes visible in your experience.

The key to engineering your Emergence is to bring *all* elements of your being—thought, feeling, words, *and actions*—into congruence with your highest vision, your true nature. This means designing your goals, plans, and actions around what is *true* within you, the emerging impulse, not what appears possible or what the world says you should or shouldn't do, even if the actions seem impractical, illogical, unreasonable, or counterintuitive. This chapter will clarify the questions of what to do and when, empowering you to take bold, inspired action (or to boldly take no action) that unlocks the "imprisoned splendor" and takes your life to a whole new level.

Before I had this terminology, my wife and I used to call the Emerging impulse a "movement." It was a feeling that something was stirring, wanting to express. It was always an adventure because the movements rarely seemed supported by external facts. We were frequently prodded toward endeavors we couldn't afford, didn't have time for, and almost never had the talent or resources readily available for. All we had was an inner sense that something more wanted to emerge and just enough faith to say yes to our yes. And as we stepped out on that invisible bridge and took actions that were congruent with our vision, our dreams manifested—from children and houses to work and travel.

The same practice has achieved equally powerful results for my clients, giving them the courage to leave jobs that no longer served them and create work that does, expand their wealth in the face of economic contraction by investing from where they *wanted to be* instead of where they were, and manifest their ideal partner by loving themselves as if they were *already* in the romance of a lifetime. Taking a page from my own drama, I've advised clients to write love letters to their imagined partner, put a place setting at the dinner table, create space in the bedroom, hug their pillow, and have out-loud conversations as if their beloved were there. It might sound crazy, but "acting out" the reality of your vision activates the visionary vibration and moves you into compelling action and brings up unconscious beliefs that are blocking you so they can be healed.

There's no limit to what you can bring forth from within when you're willing to align with this principle and then *act as if* your deepest desires are true.

The Action Paradox

Before we launch into action, I want to address the confusion that often arises in self-help and spirituality around how much action, if any, is required to bring something into form.

The fact is, for most people most of the time, action is necessary to bring things into manifestation. Virtually everything we see, feel, taste, and touch came into expression through action. But it's not always you who takes the action that brings the result. Sometimes things show up that you didn't, through physical means, directly cause. The phone rings and it's the person you had just been thinking of. You affirm that wherever you go, you find a parking space, and you pull into the crowded mall just as a car pulls out in front of you. You're sitting at your desk, struggling with an issue, and an email comes through from a friend, colleague, or advertiser with just the information you needed to make progress. "You do not need to leave your room," Franz Kafka said, describing his understanding of this principle. "Remain sitting at your table and listen. Do not even listen, simply wait, be quiet, still and solitary. The world will freely offer itself to you to be unmasked, it has no choice, it will roll in ecstasy at your feet."[2]

We've all had some version of this happen. We call it coincidence, luck, chance, a happy accident. Or, in the case of the parking space, you may even call it the power of your intention. But is that all it is? When you understand the nature of reality as a single wholeness, one infinite divine pattern forever emerging, you realize it's possible to tap into your deeper potential and watch as it materializes in ways that defy logic, bend time and space, and bust the laws of cause and effect—at least as far as we can measure them.

When a dramatic version of this happens, we call it a miracle. But a miracle is simply an instant demonstration of the perfect pattern of reality that's always here, like that radio broadcast we suddenly tune in to. When we tune in to our true nature, amazing things can happen. Opportunities show up even though we didn't seem to earn them. Bursts of creative genius arise. Healings spontaneously unfold. Lifelong traumas or dramas dissolve. Why? Because when we strip away the filters of time, space, and our false beliefs, we discover that underlying everything is pure order, harmony, and divine design.

It's important to remember, however, that *you can't plan for miracles*. Plan as if you are doing all the work and then live as if God is. That isn't to say just "go with the flow"; it means to live in the context of miracles, in a flexible, open space where something better or different than what you've planned can happen—and happen more quickly than you'd planned. The fact is, most of us, most of the time, don't live in a constant flow of instantaneous demonstrations of ultimate reality. When we experience one, it's likely to be a parking space or a book falling off a shelf, open to just the right page (which is pretty cool). But we can support the Emergence of our potential and coax out some miracles by incorporating consciously congruent actions into our everyday lifestyle. Not action as we tend to think of it (that is, trying to make something happen), but action as we've reframed it in this Emergence model—making something *welcome*.

You've probably had the experience of feeling *compelled* to do or say something, sometimes despite your better judgment or before you had time to think about it. Other times you might be hit by a burst of insight that propels you into right action. Or you might toil for hours or days on a project and then, after a period of rest, renewal, prayer, or meditation, something clicks, the resistance dissolves, and you find yourself plowing through that heretofore impossible task in a fraction of the time and energy it normally takes, having all the answers effortlessly at your fingertips. When you connect with the nature of ultimate reality within, this emerging impulse will use you as its instrument to bring the idea into expression. So it takes the form of action—but now it's *inspired* action.

It's an axiom that truth, once realized, *must* manifest. Sometimes it shows up at your door, sometimes it shoves you out the door, and sometimes it makes you sit down and shut up, which will turn out to be exactly what was needed for the next step to emerge. That's why the foundation of this work is to gain a deeper realization of oneness with our true nature and purpose. The clearer that is, the more effortless our actions become, and the less action it takes to bring about results. We're no longer working on something; *something* is working on us—and ultimately through and *as* us.

The Seven Rules of Right Action

While there are many roads to becoming a master of right action, the following seven-rule structure has been effective in my private practice with people from many walks of life:

1. Have a Clear Vision

2. Act Like Your Vision Is True

3. Act According to Your Highest Beliefs

4. Act from Where You Want to Be, Not from Where You Are

5. Act from Who You Want to Be, Not from How You Feel

6. Act without Concern for the Results

7. Act from the Stillness

When these rules guide the way you act in the world, not only is your Emergence activated but your actions also operate as a rite of purification, dissolving the ego's resistance. And as you become increasingly free of the ego's agenda and become a clearer channel of the divine impulse, your actions become an extension of the cosmic dance itself.

Let's start learning the dance steps to the life of your dreams.

Have a Clear Vision

In Stage One, we did a deep dive around having a clear vision for your larger purpose. But in the context of creating right action in every area of your life, you can practice having a vision for whatever you're doing. In this way, you create a visionary mind-set that constantly activates your creative potential. Whether it's working on a new career opportunity, building a relationship, going on a trip, going on a date, or just going to the store, there's great power in taking at least a few moments to get clear on your highest vision and deepest intention for what lies ahead.

Tapping into, defining, and even declaring your ideal outcomes pulls you out of the inertia of mental and emotional trends—within and around you—and puts you back at the center, at the cause. The simple practice of starting each day, each project, or each event with a clear vision, rooted in your core values and larger purpose, can set a tone and create the conditions for clearer guidance and inspired action. It gives you a kind of immunity from many of the common challenges that throw people off course and lets you operate at an optimal level.

Act Like Your Vision Is True

When the titular character in Shakespeare's *Hamlet* says, "Suit the action to the word, the word to the action," he is talking about how to perform a scene from a play, but he just as easily could be talking about how to behave in this divine drama called life. Put another way: walk your talk. As we've been discussing, the key to powerful action is to align it with your highest vision. Just as saying an affirmation can help embody a new level of consciousness, your actions can be *moving affirmations* that ground that consciousness in your nervous system, in the neural pathways of your brain, in the very marrow of your bones.

It's as if there's an invisible bridge between where we are and where we want to be, but it doesn't appear beneath our feet until we step out onto it, like in the movie *Indiana Jones and the Last Crusade* when Jones is faced with a deep chasm he must cross—"The Path of God"—to save his father's life, but the only way across is to take a "leap of faith." This is not just the universe providing us with an arbitrary challenge; it's intended to strengthen our connection with the invisible source within, making it as real to us as the world we see with our senses, which in turn allows us to feel more empowered in the face of limited conditions.

We can mindfully develop this inner connection by taking steps every day across that invisible bridge. They can be baby steps at first—having a challenging conversation with a colleague or making a small purchase that supports our vision but won't break the bank. Every day will bring some opportunity to take another step, and it's important that we seize it. Unless we actively engage this process, we'll remain on one side of the chasm, with our dreams on the other.

Another benefit to using our actions as living affirmations is that we take the pressure off needing to see immediate results for anything we do, just as we don't expect to say an affirmation and have our life magically change. We do the inner work to cultivate the soil of our soul, to make it fertile for the seed of potential to emerge. Likewise, when you frame actions in the same way, you'll do things that are congruent with your vision, without trying to force something to happen. And as a result, your actions will be purer, free of resistance, and carry more power.

It's the mystical version of "fake it till you make it." "Faking" in this case is just a way of rehearsing for what's trying to emerge, preparing your mental, emotional, spiritual, and sometimes physical structures to be able to express the next level. Since every day our experiences and actions prepare us for the next, we're always, in a sense, rehearsing for *something*, whether consciously or unconsciously. It's up to us to rehearse the highest and purest version of our Self. As Kurt Vonnegut said, "We are what we pretend to be, so we must be careful about what we pretend to be."[3] You are the light of the world, a unique expression of infinite love and power; when you act like anything less than that, you're pretending to be something you're not.

Are you rehearsing the role of a valuable, worthy, and abundant spiritual being, acting in a hero's or heroine's journey, or are you taking the part of a weak, broken, poor human being and hobbling along in that story? Are you pretending to be a confident visionary being with a mighty mission to fulfill, boldly springing forward from that perspective, or are you pretending to be a confused, inadequate person who doesn't have a meaningful reason to live . . . and are you coping at that level of consciousness? We get to choose what play we're in and what part we'll play.

Which story are you going to star in?

This week, pay attention to the divine drama you're acting in. Is it a role you consciously chose? Does it match the vision you have for your life, what you want to create, the person you want to be? By bringing awareness to your circumstances and behavior, you'll begin to notice areas where you want to see change—and in some cases even begin to see change happening. If you want to accelerate your Emergence, identify an area where you can align your actions more with the vision, creating an *affirmation in action*—that is, an action that matches the kind of person you would be if you were living your vision. Then practice that a little each day for at least the next week. If fear or resistance come up, embrace them. Be gentle with yourself, but stay the course. (We'll work more deeply on what's coming up in Stage Six: Embrace What Appears Broken.)

Act According to Your Highest Beliefs

Many sincere people interested in self-help and spirituality claim to believe the core concepts in this material—that there really is a God and each of us is an expression of this divine loving intelligence. They might even be able to talk eloquently on the subject and quote from the latest books in the category. But if you observed them, without knowing their beliefs, you would see few signs of this truth manifest in their lives. In the areas that matter most to them, they don't *act* like people who believe they're connected to an infinite source of safety, support, and supply. And that gap between what they say they believe and how they behave might as well be infinite, because until it's bridged, real Emergence is nearly impossible.

Sometimes beliefs can become a comfort zone that keeps us from facing our deeper perceptions and taking the difficult actions that would transform us. And it's only through the alchemical process of turning beliefs into action that truth becomes a living reality rather than just a nice philosophy. This was a rude awakening for me when, after years of studying and practicing, not only was I not getting the results I wanted but things were getting worse. As I began to look honestly at what I "believed" versus how I acted, I had to confess that there was quite a chasm; I didn't *really* believe what I said. I just liked the *idea* of believing and the feeling it gave me to believe I believed it!

Do you want to know what you *really* believe so you can start from a place of honesty and authenticity and build upon that foundation? Don't merely look at what you're thinking, saying, affirming, or praying; look at what you're *doing*, especially under pressure. If your actions are not in integrity with what you profess to believe in, you'll suffer and become stagnant. In fact, if you're currently struggling in an area where you have a great deal of "positive belief," that's a likely sign that you're not congruent in that area. In order to move to the next level, you must align your actions with your highest beliefs about God, life, and your true Self. Then the next level of the journey will emerge.

Years ago, I wanted to grow my business but was waiting for circumstances to become more "favorable" before I took the next step.

I was visualizing, affirming, and beating my chest with belief, but conditions continued to decline. In frustration, I visited my spiritual mentor, looking for reassurance and moral support. What I got instead was a challenge. He asked me what I would do *if I believed* all the spiritual truths I espoused—that life was abundant and God supported me. I began to explain how my rent was due and mumbled some sad story about being unsupported as a child, but he cut me off without sympathy, telling me he wasn't interested in my tales of woe. He asked the question again: "What would you *do* if you really believed all this stuff?" I protested that he didn't understand; I had bills to pay, an uncertain outcome to this investment, and a fiancée to stay engaged to! Again, he stopped me short and said that if I didn't act according to what I professed to believe, especially all that I was praying, affirming, and visualizing, then I was out of integrity with myself and would continue to suffer.

I felt confronted, hurt, even a little pissed. But I knew he was right. I was praying out of both sides of my mouth, affirming that life was abundant on one side and making up reasons why I couldn't move forward on the other. Gandhi, whose name, to many, is synonymous with integrity, said, "To believe in something, and not to live it, is dishonest."[4] I was living a lie in regard to my own values. My lack of integrity was preventing me from holding the energy necessary to manifest my vision. Like a house that lacks structural integrity and collapses under its own weight, my inner house was divided and could not stand. After a little more suffering, I took the leap, said yes to my yes, and made the investment in my vision. It was scary to write that check. But it was an exciting kind of scary— that mix of fear and exhilaration, which is often a sign you're on to something. In the first month, I made the money back. In the second month, I made *ten times* my initial investment. And I never looked back to that old level. But it wasn't just more money that emerged; more of *me* came with it.

ACT AS IF YOU'RE IT   111

One definition of integrity is to align your beliefs, words, and actions with each other—to be whole and undivided. But this is relative integrity, because you could believe life is hard (even though in reality it isn't) and then struggle in accordance with that belief, becoming exhausted, burned out, and disillusioned. Another definition of integrity is to be moral, ethical, and honest. But you can be a moral, ethical, honest person who, according to your cultural beliefs, would never pursue your deepest desire. The truest sense of integrity, however, is about being congruent with your soul's purpose, your real nature and being, which may be in opposition to your cultural, parental, or societal beliefs and values. That's why many visionary leaders have been seen as heretics, lunatics, or worse.

Living at this level of integrity requires faith—the *substance* of things hoped for, the *evidence* of things not seen. Real faith is not just "belief"; it's a *knowing* that comes from living more by insight than eyesight; it's an actual *contact* with reality, a soul-sense that is developed as you act from your belief, from your inner vision, and experience the reward. Every time you do, you strengthen your ability to step out on that invisible bridge—to live from the inside out—until you're able to walk in this world, unshakable and unstoppable.

If you're ready to turn your belief into a fiery faith, identify one area where you think you have an empowering belief but you're not getting the results you want. Then ask yourself, "If I really believed (fill in the blank), how would I act in this situation?" Contemplate how you would hold yourself, how you would talk, and what you would do if you *really* believed this. Be still and listen for the guidance. Then honor it as best you can. Remember, this is a practice that gets stronger over time. It's not practice that makes perfect; it's the practice of perfection, of the higher ideals. Be kind to yourself, be patient, and keep practicing.

Act from Where You Want to Be,
Not from Where You Are

Although an ability to problem solve is considered a good quality to have, it's often an obstacle to the solution. The urge to correct something is a form of resistance to what is, and what you resist persists. When you wrestle with a problem, you vibrate at the same frequency as the problem and remain stuck. Problems are symptoms of a particular state of consciousness and will always exist at that level, the same way water will always be ice at thirty-two degrees Fahrenheit. You can't solve the problem of frozen water as long as you're living at thirty-two degrees. But rise above that temperature and the ice melts.

Problems aren't solved; they dissolve as you evolve.

To evolve, we must take our attention off the problem and place it on the opportunity. We must rise above being merely a problem solver and become a vision holder. This requires us to act based on where we want to go (our vision), not where we are (the problem). The same principle applies to driving a car. When you lose control of the vehicle and it's skidding toward an obstacle, the tendency is to look where you *don't* want to go, as if that'll help you avoid it. But that will actually cause you to run right into it! Instead, you must focus on where you *want* to go, because the hands naturally follow the eyes, causing you to course-correct out of the skid. The same is true when your life is careening out of control. Rather than focusing on the obstacle, you need to look beyond it to where you *want* to go. And because energy flows where your attention goes, it will cause you to think, say, and do things that put you back on the road to success.

But more than just avoiding our problems or mitigating their impact, acting from where we want to be is about becoming a candidate for the larger life trying to emerge. A chronic problem is often a symptom that we're living in a world that no longer fits us.

Something bigger is trying to emerge, but our focus on where we are instead of where we want to be keeps us contracted mentally, emotionally, and physically, and the larger life can't squeeze through. The energy not only gets stuck and starts to wreak havoc but we remain small, followers instead of leaders, victims instead of victors, whiners instead of winners. We wrestle with our environment, trying to get energy *from* it, when we are divine power plants designed to generate it.

When we focus on where we're going, on the vision, and live as if we're already there, rather than trying to get there, we don't just draw that reality toward us; we create it. As a result, we find ourselves more often in the right place at the right time because that's where we're already living. "I skate to where the puck *is going to be*," renowned hockey player Wayne Gretzky said, "not where it has been."[5] This is acting from insight, not eyesight; being at cause, not at effect. This is living a visionary life.

Look at a problem you've been struggling to solve or an area where you've been trying to *avoid* a problem (which means your attention is still on it, even if unconsciously, keeping you stuck at the level of the problem). If you're using this book to work on your big vision, you can work with some challenging aspect of that. Ask yourself, "Where do I want to go in this area? What outcome do I want?" Imagine yourself in that reality, having that result, and ask, "How would I act from this place? Who would I be? How would I talk? What would I do?" Notice the ideas that arise. For example, maybe you're struggling with money problems, and when you imagine not having those problems anymore and ask what you would do from that improved place, you discover you would "have more fun," "write more," "take dancing lessons," or finally "have that conversation with (fill in the blank)" you've been avoiding.

Over the next two weeks, shift your focus to taking one or more of these actions instead of wrestling with your current condition, and watch what new energy and insights emerge. Because the problem can't exist at a higher frequency, as you start acting from this new vibrational place, you might find yourself running right into the very solution you've been searching for.

Act from Who You Want to Be, Not from How You Feel

You may have been raised by parents who encouraged you to express your feelings, only to be told in school or at work that you must repress them. Or maybe you studied self-help teachings that told you to honor your emotions, only to find yourself in a relationship where you didn't feel safe to express them. Bottom line: there's a lot of confusion around how much "say" we should give our emotions. The solution is to be in tune with them but never to become a slave to them.

Many people believe that if they don't "feel like it," that's a legitimate reason not to act. But it's no reason at all; it's an unexamined false belief. It also shows up in less obvious but equally pernicious self-talk like, "I'm just not inspired," or "I don't have the energy." Letting our feelings determine our actions is called emotional reasoning. It's a cognitive distortion that makes us believe that what we feel is true just because we feel it. Then these feelings are used to rationalize (i.e., tell rational lies about) why we don't act. Culturally, it's a common pact we make: "If you let me have the excuse of not feeling like it, I'll let you have it too."

But that's not how we do things around here.

In the Emergence model, we let the truth about ourselves determine our feelings and our vision determine our actions.

Taking action despite your feelings, particularly fear, is called courage. But the saying "feel the fear and do it anyway" could be equally applied to all feelings: "Feel like you don't want to do it and do it anyway." "Feel uninspired and do it anyway." "Feel unworthy and do it anyway." I've used the do-it-anyway strategy with my clients for years. A client will say, "I couldn't work on my project today because I wasn't inspired," often adding a dramatic flourish like, "I was just paralyzed. I couldn't bring myself to do it!" My response will be something like, "Wow, that sounds horrible. What was it like to be paralyzed, unable to bring yourself to do it? Was it painful? How did the paramedics finally get your limbs moving again?"

They usually get the joke and realize they're creating scary stories and fearful images in their mind to give them an out. Then when I ask them to do whatever they were "too paralyzed" to do—whether it's coming up with some ideas for a project, putting together the first step in their plan, or jogging in place—always, without fail, they're able to do it. It's often a powerful moment of awareness when they realize that their feelings were *not* stopping them. When they *act* like an inspired person and work on the project even when they feel empty, they activate inspiration. When they act like a confident person and take bold action even when they feel scared, they activate confidence. And when they act like an energized person and exercise even when they feel tired, they activate energy.

When we "do it anyway," we have a direct experience that shows that we really are the source of power in our life. Regardless of what we feel, we can use action, based on our vision, as a tool to create any feeling we need. As Ralph Waldo Emerson said, "Do the thing and you will be given the power."[6]

Brian was a client of mine who had been struggling to write his book. After coming to a session with a well-rehearsed set of reasons why he hadn't fulfilled his weekly writing goal, I took him through this process and, within moments, had him writing passionately. He laughed as he realized how clever his mind was at keeping him stuck and how potentially easy it was to get free again. I brought the point home with another question: "If it wasn't your feelings that stopped you, why didn't you write?" After he expressed a variety of reasons,

I answered simply, "Because you didn't *do it*. That's it. You didn't write because you didn't write. There's no bigger reason, no karmic payback, no inner-child sabotage." He still seemed unsure about his ability to follow through, convinced that there must be some deeper issue. So I asked a coaching question I use to get leverage on people's emotions: "If the life of someone you cared about depended on your completing this—legally and ethically—in the allotted time, would you find the will and the way to do it?" There was an instant shift in his energy. The excuses evaporated, and by the time we were finished, he was a man on a mission.

Where did that energy come from? Did he suddenly heal the emotional, astrological, numerological issues that had prevented him from acting earlier? No. His parents still didn't appreciate him enough, his boss still didn't respect him enough, his kids still didn't listen to him, and Mercury was still in retrograde! He even had many of the same worries, doubts, and fears. But somehow now he was ready to act. Why? Because what you think and feel can only determine what you do *if you let it*.

On their own, *your thoughts and feelings have no power*.

You can always take the next step, even if all that means is lacing up your shoes, powering up your computer, or picking up the phone.

Then you can take the next step . . . and the next.

Your feelings are important and they have their place. Process them, embrace them, get to know the deeper beliefs and stories generating them. This will ultimately yield rich insights that will awaken greater potential and add more meaning to your life. (In fact, we'll be doing just that in Stage Six: Embrace What Appears Broken.) Your feelings are also part of an important guidance system. But they don't tell you what's true; they tell you what you believe. And your beliefs don't tell you what's true; they tell you what your best guess about reality is, which is always relative and often misleading.

Feel your feelings. Give them their due. But don't give your feelings command over your actions. If you have a goal and a plan and they're rooted in your core values and aligned with your higher vision, act accordingly *even when you don't feel like it*. Then, as part of your plan, take the time to work with your feelings. This way you get to be emotionally healthy *and* actualize your potential. If all you ever do is cater to your feelings, you get neither. You get stuck in an endless loop of emotional reasoning, full of rational lies about why you can't create the life you truly desire, the life that is trying to emerge in you.

Look at an area where you're not making progress or where you want to accelerate things and identify where your decisions are based on how you feel rather than on what you want. Are you trying to lose weight but don't *feel* like exercising and letting that be a good reason not to? Is there some project you want to start or finish but just don't *feel* inspired, so you don't do it? If you want to take your practice to the next level, pick one of these areas where you've been struggling and *commit* to doing it for the next thirty days, no matter what. Notice how often your feelings tempt you to slow down, back off, or give up. Be aware of how real the excuses feel. If they seem like core issues, you can do the work from Stage Six in the next chapter—*but keep taking the actions anyway*. After a month, reassess your emotional threshold in this area and recognize the ways you've grown more resilient.

Act without Concern for the Results

When our actions don't bring the results we want, we often quit as an employee of the universe and try to become manager of it. We think we know better what should happen and when. But our finite mind can't begin to grasp the infinite intelligence that created everything. The same universal love that put fish in the sea, fruit on the trees, and governs all in perfect order is also running our life. It knows what we need and has our best interests at heart (since we are, after all, expressions of it). One of the hardest truths to accept is that while we may control the actions, the universe controls the results.

When we try to control results, we impose our finite concepts onto an infinite idea, greatly limiting it. Neither acorn nor caterpillar would think to control its own emergence, and the divine result is far greater than either could have imagined. As we surrender to this divine design and allow it to unfold through us, there may be points along the way when we find our current state wanting. But we must stay the course.

We take congruent actions *because it's who we are*; it's our authentic nature. If you're a writer, you write and do whatever else the writer's life entails, even when you're unsure the writing is read or appreciated. If you're a teacher, you teach, whether faced with eager students or not. A flower blossoms because that's its nature. It doesn't do it so someone will notice it, appreciate it, or wear it on a corsage. It doesn't wilt due to a lack of acknowledgment. It keeps on flowering, giving away its perfume, opening to the light.

This doesn't mean that you ignore whatever results you're getting. Remaining unattached to results is not the same as ignoring them. Results are feedback. And feedback is valuable. Since the world conforms to your consciousness, what you experience outside—particularly what pushes or pulls you—is a reflection of what's inside. So if things don't seem to be working as planned, it might mean you should take another look inside and possibly make some adjustments to your actions. If you want to be a singer and every time you sing, dogs howl and babies cry, it's not necessarily a sign that you should give up your dream of the Grand Ole Opry, but it might be a sign you should get some lessons or listen more deeply to the song you're really meant to sing. If your latest marketing campaign is resulting in too few sales, that might not mean you should stop selling, but it might mean you should get clearer on *what* you're selling, *why* you're selling it, and *who* you're selling it to.

Align your actions with your vision and act from that place of already being/having the thing you're moving toward—without concern for the outcome. Then assess the results and see if the feedback resonates. Does it bring up unresolved emotions or limited beliefs? Use that information to refine your intention and vision, which will propel you into more powerful action. Action rooted in vision, without attachment to results, is the most powerful action. There's no resistance, no separation. In Eugen Herrigel's classic book *Zen in the Art of Archery*, the archer reaches a state of mind where the arrow is already in the bull's-eye before it leaves the bow. From that state, it's impossible to miss. Likewise, when your actions come from this place of engaged nonattachment, the result is already in the action before the action is taken. As Krishna states in the Bhagavad Gita, "Abandon all attachment to the results of action and attain supreme peace."[7]

To practice this nonattachment, find an area where you've been stressing over the results and ask yourself, "If I weren't concerned about the results here, how would I approach this? What would I do differently, more of, or less of?" Then apply that guidance to the work at hand. And if you want a slightly more advanced version of this, ask yourself, "If I weren't concerned with results at all, what would I do *that I'm not currently doing*, and how would I do it?" Then take on that challenge.

Act from the Stillness

With all this talk of action, it might seem like you should always be in motion or you'll be out of integrity. This couldn't be further from the truth. Sometimes the most affirmative and courageous action is no action. It's having an impulse to defend yourself, prove a point, or make someone else wrong but choosing to be silent, simply witnessing that energy, starving it of its power. It's having that obsessive urge to send another nervous email or make a compulsive phone call to convince a customer to buy from you or someone to date you but choosing instead to delete the email, put down the phone, become still, and feel your way back to the center of your abundant being. It's that project or job you *don't* pursue out of fear of needing the money so you can create space for the work you're meant to do. "One who sees inaction in action and action in inaction," said Krishna in the Bhagavad Gita, "is intelligent among men."[8] These moments of silent inaction are loaded with transformational potential that can neutralize lifelong patterns, uncover new layers of character, and set your life on a whole new course.

As the saying goes, "Don't just do something; sit there." Sometimes we need to sit on our hands until a wave of anxiety or compulsivity passes. If you've ever practiced this kind of inaction, you know it is anything but inactive. I used to practice this kind of time-out whenever I felt myself becoming too anxiously active. I would take a day off to meditate and do only what felt inspired, and then go back into meditation. Every time I took this kind of intentional break, my life would go to a new level.

It was a form of fasting from the mind's fear-based motives. When you do this, you dissolve the limited beliefs—like uprooting the weeds of your mind and freeing that energy to feed the seeds of your potential. And like all mindful meditation, as you practice this regularly, whether it's stopping for a moment, an hour, a day, or a longer retreat, it has a transferring effect in your everyday interactions. Someone cuts in front of you on the freeway and triggers a reaction within you. But instead of engaging it, you find yourself dropping back into conscious inaction and observing it. Because you didn't fuel that old pattern, a piece of your ego gets chipped away and a little karma gets burned up. This is effortless Emergence, the path of awakening.

This week, notice instances where your actions seem to be coming from a fearful or frenetic place, where you're pushing or trying to make something happen, and practice a little inaction. It might mean listening more than you speak, checking your email only once an hour or (gasp!) once a day, cutting your to-do list in half, or, if your tendency is to never unplug, taking a whole day off to do nothing productive at all (except perhaps praying and meditating). Journal about what comes up in the absence of action. Notice the feelings you may have been avoiding through possibly compulsive behaviors, and take the time to feel them fully. Like any fast, this can be detoxifying, bringing old stuff to the surface. So be kind and caring with yourself. Drink lots of water. If things get really shaky, take a relaxing salt bath or a walk. And if deeper core material surfaces, jump ahead and try working with the exercises in Stage Six.

The Curse of "Can't"

Just as there's no such thing as being stuck, there's no such thing as "can't." "Can't" is just a filter the ego puts up to stop your growth. It's a limited belief and has no power over you.

Notice where that idea hit you. Did it make you say, "Yes!" or did you find yourself arguing for your limitations? The latter response is the "victim" shadow rearing its head—that powerless part of us that hasn't been fully understood and integrated (something we'll address in Stage Six: Embrace What Appears Broken). Its survival depends on the story of can't. One of the most powerful Emergence questions to ask when you hit this threshold is, "How *can* I?" This realigns you with your deeper truth and allows you to uncover actions that are congruent with your vision.

But let me qualify what I mean when I say there's no such thing as "can't." There may be certain things you can't do now, or maybe ever. If I wanted to dunk a basketball, I'd have to admit that I don't have a lot of natural ability at shooting baskets, let alone dunking. But saying that I can't *right now* isn't being a victim; saying "I can't" and giving up *is*. It's also a lie because there's no way for me to know whether I truly can't before I've given it everything I can. Even then, there's always something more I *can* do. Thomas Edison could've said "I can't" after a thousand attempts to create the lightbulb (let alone ten thousand attempts, which he reportedly tried before succeeding). And most people would've agreed because most people stop after the first few attempts. But for every example of someone saying "I can't" and stopping, there are many examples of someone who said "I can" and kept going. If you want something badly enough, *that's a clue that it's already in you*, which means there's always something more you *can* do, something more you can become, another action you *can* take to create the right conditions for its Emergence.

When you say you can't, what you're really saying the majority of the time is "I won't." If you're willing to acknowledge that, you're one step closer to being unstuck or becoming free of the perception of being stuck, since "stuck" is a state of mind. Then you can ask, "Why won't I?" and discover what's really stopping you, because it's not the circumstance. *It's never the circumstance.* No matter how far from your destination, you can always take another step in its direction, even if that step takes place in your mind first, then your emotions, then your body. *There's always a next step.* "There are many ways of going forward," Franklin Roosevelt said, "but only one way of standing still."[9]

So look at that one area of your life where you're most convinced you're stuck and hear yourself saying, "I can't." Then change it to "I won't"—and ask why. "I can't start this business" becomes "I won't start this business, because . . . I'm afraid of failing . . . I don't have the money . . . I'm afraid nobody will buy my stuff . . . I'm afraid people will judge me . . . It's going to be so hard, I'm afraid

I won't have any time for my family . . ." While this may be painful at first, it's the first step toward freedom. At least then you'll know what beliefs you're using to hold yourself back. Then you can apply the tools in this book to embrace what seems broken (which we'll get to in the next chapter) and know where you must cultivate more congruent conditions.

As stated earlier, one of the quickest ways to break free from what you can't do is to focus on what you *can* do. "I am only one, but I am one," said Edward Everett Hale.[10] "I cannot do everything, but I can do something. And I will not let what I cannot do interfere with what I can do." The act of asking "What *can* I do?" in whatever situation you're facing will open you up to another level of wisdom. You may bump up against more stories of why you "can't," but if you keep asking, you'll tune in to that inner wisdom and receive new energy and ideas. The answers are always broadcasting within you; you simply need to find the station they're playing on and they will manifest, and you will have your manifest-station!

The Cost of Inaction

As Thoreau observed, the sad fact of the human experience is that most people lead lives of quiet desperation, never saying yes to the yes within them, waiting for some perfect or safe condition to finally act upon their deepest desires—a condition that never comes. It can't, because it won't come *to* them; rather, it must come *through* them. This doesn't just lead to an unlived life; it leads to many of the problems that plague people. When we don't honor the emerging impulse within us, we withhold gifts from our friends, family, and the rest of the world. Think of all the inventions, breakthrough ideas, transformational wisdom, and timeless masterpieces that never find their way into expression because an individual who was born to express them did not act. The cures for everything that ails us—and the inspiration for creating a life beyond our wildest dreams—are right now sitting in the consciousness of humanity, like seeds waiting to germinate, waiting for those courageous enough to cultivate the conditions for their emergence.

So the question is, what's inside you wanting to emerge?

Where are you withholding the gifts you came here to give, the gifts you are obliged to share? Just as every part of a cell exists to serve the greater good of the body, all you possess within you is for the greater good of the planet. That's not to say you aren't meant to enjoy it—you are, and thoroughly—but there's no way to experience the fullness of your being and the fulfillment of your heart and soul without living, giving, *and acting* from your highest vision. Will it be scary or difficult to go for it? Will you, like Edison, stumble a few times before succeeding? Perhaps. But just as walking is really controlled falling, success is controlled failing. It's how we evolve. And at the end of one's life, it's rarely the things we've tried and failed that haunt us—it's the things we never tried at all.

Take the chance. You have nothing to lose except a life of mediocrity. As Oliver Wendell Holmes said, "Alas for those that never sing. But die with all their music in them."[11]

Let the music in you live.

It only takes one note at a time, and before you know it, you're singing.

STAGE SIX

EMBRACE WHAT
APPEARS BROKEN

There is no coming to consciousness without pain.

CARL GUSTAV JUNG

Silhouetted against the glimmering gold and crimson sun reflected in the Great Lake, a solitary jack pine stands amongst ancient rocks and burgeoning new growth, its branches bowed but unbroken. Having taken root on these hostile shores where other trees dared not, it is one of the few survivors of a recent wildfire and a symbol of vulnerability and endurance. Where other species might fail to thrive in these harsh climes, the jack pine, with its wind-warped and fire-scorched limbs, continues to adapt and refuses to surrender.[1]

A "fire tree," the jack has a special kinship with its blistering brother. Unlike many other trees, it doesn't release all its seeds as they mature but protects them for years—even decades—in thick, hard serotinous cones glued shut by a strong resin. Only one thing can force this tree to yield its hidden fruit and allow its natural evolution: fire. And when it finally comes, sweeping through the forest, the flames ascend to the tree's crown, their searing heat melting the resin and opening the scales of the cones to release its progeny.

But the transformation by fire doesn't stop there. The blaze, having burned away much of the forest floor, clears the site and

prepares the seedbed for the newly fallen seedlings. And as it continues to swirl through the jack pine's world, it consumes the old,
diseased trees and plants, reducing competition for the new life and
creating a path for its emergence.

Scorching everything to the ground, the dance of the jack pine
and its fiery foe reveals that the wrath and renewal of rebirth are one.

Problems Are Answered Prayers

The universe is not neutral. It has a plan, a pattern, an evolutionary
idea seeking willing places for its ever-expanding expression. Because
of this, even in the midst of seeming chaos and destruction, it's conspiring for our freedom and preparing the seedbed of our soul for
something more to emerge. But to benefit, we must become what
businessman and new-thought author W. Clement Stone was pur-
portedly described as an "inverse paranoid," someone who believes
that life is plotting *for* us.[2]

This is rarely how we live. We often resist this Emerging
impulse—or urge to Emerge—because we're afraid of change. To the
ego, change is equivalent to danger, even death, because part of it
must often be burned down for something new to be born. Denying
this evolutionary call, however, causes an inner pressure that must
find outlet, sometimes in destructive ways, breaking out as disease,
financial collapse, or relationship meltdown, among many unpleas-
ant possibilities.

But the meaning of these events isn't that we're being punished or
that someone's to blame. These challenges are wake-up calls, telling
us we've settled for a life too small and must open up our tightly held
places to a larger vision. As the Gospel of Thomas says, "If you bring
forth what is within you, it will save you. If you do not bring forth
what is within you, it will destroy you."[3] Just as the jack pine requires
a fire to burn away the glue that keeps its seeds from falling, crises

burn away our limited self-concepts, allowing our deeper nature to unfold. As this chapter intends to show, our suffering carries the seeds of our salvation, our problems contain the answers to our prayers, and our darkness is a womb where our greater light is born.

But activating this light requires that we embrace our shadow, and realizing our wholeness requires us to become big enough to hold our brokenness. This is a core condition we must cultivate for our full Emergence. And this takes us to the heart of our greatest struggle: we've been brought up to believe we must resist, fight, or destroy seemingly negative forces or that we must repair, control, or repress our deficiencies. But your darkness is not the enemy; it is the rich soil you must dig into and be immersed in before something new can break through the surface. Just as certain plants need to struggle in rocky soil to toughen their bark, strengthen their roots, and thrive, the sometimes-rocky process of embracing and integrating the wounded or lacking parts of yourself—instead of trying to heal or improve them—activates in you things you need to flourish. The more you expose and redeem the dark and seemingly deficient places within you, the more bountiful your harvest will be.

In short, *embracing what appears broken* is about taking the truth you've been learning, that there's nothing wrong with you, and making it a *living experience*, freeing you from a lifetime of struggle and shame and introducing you to the one true love of your life: you.

A Conspiracy of Good

The first part of this new healing paradigm is accepting *everything* as a supportive element on your path of awakening and fulfillment. This means that no matter what the situation appears to be, you name it good and embrace it in gratitude. Not just once or twice or now and again but as a way of life. Why? Because the truth is that there's only one life, one power governing everything, and its nature is absolute good. Harmony and wholeness already is. But you can only experience this truth to the extent that it's an active part of your consciousness. It's not "I'll believe it when I see it"; it's "You'll see it when you believe it." You don't experience reality; you experience your perception of it—a relative projection of infinite perfection. By declaring everything good, you align yourself with "the way it really is," activate this deeper soul-sense, and progressively see that everything *is* good, until that new perception becomes your improved experience.

The story of Joseph—found in the Quran, Torah, and the Old Testament—is a great example of this paradigm. He turned every problem into a seed of greater potential. He was sold into slavery by his brothers, framed by the woman of the house where he worked, and then put in prison for a crime he never committed. Situation after situation, he faced adversity and obstacles that would cause most people to give up and wallow in resentment. But he kept bringing his attention back to the vision God had given him—a vision that seemed impossible in his lowly stature—and embraced what was in front of him, looking for how he could grow from each experience. This caused him to rise to the top, wherever he was, whether as slave or prisoner.

Ultimately Joseph's journey led him to interpret the pharaoh's dream, which prophesied a coming famine. Heeding this, the pharaoh stored food and, when the famine came to pass, it saved the people. The pharaoh named Joseph his right hand, making him the second most powerful man in the land—the fulfillment of Joseph's vision. Joseph's brothers were eventually brought before him, sure to suffer harsh punishment. But Joseph held no grudge and forgave them. It wasn't "You did a bad thing and you're really bad guys, but I'm better than that." That's not true forgiveness. True forgiveness is the realization that no error was ever committed, that no harm was ever done. Joseph understood this when he said, "You intended to harm me, but God intended it all for good. He brought me to this position so I could save the lives of many people" (Genesis 50:20). He caught the bigger picture. If his brothers hadn't sold him into slavery and he hadn't gone through his trials, he wouldn't have been there to interpret the dream and save the land from famine.

Everything is conspiring for your good, awakening your deeper potential, and preparing you for greater things, whether it's meant to land you on the front page of the paper or the front porch of a neighbor in need. But to harvest the blessings of your journey, you must practice this awareness, reinterpreting everything you see until you see the divine conspiracy everywhere.

The Divine Drama

There is only one all-loving, all-giving intelligence unfolding a perfect pattern of infinite potential. Where there's resistance to this, it appears as a crisis, a conflict, or an enemy to contend with. This includes the enemies within you—that cast of characters that seem broken, evil, unworthy, and in need of being healed, fixed, or disposed of. As a storyteller, I understand that the obstacles and challenges I put my characters through are there to activate and express their deeper dimensions so they can become the hero/heroine of their story and illuminate the deeper themes—the story's message. *I design that into the story*. It's the mechanics of drama.

The same mechanism is at work in our lives. We are actively participating in a divine drama. As Shakespeare wrote in *As You Like It*, "All the world's a stage and all the men and women merely players."[4] The problem is that we identify with the part we're playing (the personality/ego) and the play we're in (the story) rather than with the author who wrote it (higher wisdom) and the actor playing it (higher Self). When we interact, we don't meet each other; we meet the characters we're playing, causing what Michael Bernard Beckwith calls "the friction of the fictions." We react, judge, and create stories about the story, building beliefs of betrayal, rejection, victimization, and good versus evil, which keep us in constant struggle. Then through the Law of Mind (which turns our beliefs into experience), we perpetuate, exacerbate, and magnify the very thing we're trying to change or get rid of. But when you understand you're starring in this divine production for the evolution of your soul, you realize you're not a victim of circumstance. You cocreated this play and cast the characters. You designed this drama on earth's stage, and people are playing their part so you can play yours.

This may feel 180 degrees away from what your intuition tells you—that there really are bad things and bad people and you need to fight them and fix them, including all the bad things in you. Maybe it sounds like relativistic thinking that makes everything equal and thus everything meaningless. To be clear, the fact that everything is conspiring for your good does *not* mean you should condone destructive actions or do without compassion for the pain you or others experience. Far from it. But if you fight these things, you will fuel them. You'll stay stuck in the drama, believing you're the character you're playing, misunderstanding the divine author's intention for the play, and never experiencing the powerful transformation of a true hero's (or heroine's) journey.

Antoinette Tuff, the bookkeeper at Ronald E. McNair Discovery Learning Academy in Decatur, Georgia, was one such heroine. When twenty-year-old Michael Hill walked into her school of more than eight hundred children, armed with an AK-47-style assault rifle, five hundred rounds of ammunition, and "nothing to live for," and took Tuff hostage; what could have been another tragic school shooting became the scene of a modern-day miracle.

Tuff didn't deny the play she was in, but she didn't get stuck in the drama. Anchored by her deep spiritual life, she was able to see through the appearances of a "bad guy"—even beyond her own immediate survival—and negotiate with Hill and emergency services over the phone. "We're not going to hate you," she assured Hill, calling him "sweetie" and "baby" and eventually telling him, "I love you. I'm proud of you. We all go through something in life. You're gonna be okay, sweetheart." She seemed intent not only on saving the children from Hill but also saving Hill from himself. And as she kept the police at a distance, she tried to get closer to him. She saw herself in Hill and, rather than judging him, she empathized and confessed, "I tried to commit suicide last year after my husband left me."[5]

Hill finally gave up his weapon and surrendered.

Poised from a practice of prayer, forgiveness, and self-awareness, Tuff was able to speak from a place of vulnerability that built real rapport, turned hopelessness into possibility, convinced a mentally unstable man to relinquish his weapon and ultimately lie down in surrender, without ever throwing a punch, firing a shot, or even raising her voice. After the Newtown, Connecticut, school shooting of 2012, the executive vice president of the National Rifle Association insisted, "The only thing that stops a bad guy with a gun is a good guy with a gun."[6] But Tuff's results proved that guns are not the only solution. A person armed with faith, a belief in a greater power, and the courage to live from that place can not only cause a man to lay down his weapon but also help him open up his heart. Tuff stepped out of the limited story of society, even the story of herself, and was able to act from a higher, more all-embracing "true story." The result was to turn a potential tragedy into triumph; the result was a *new story*.

This chapter has a dual purpose: to shift you from the pain of fighting and fixing to the peace of loving and accepting, and to encourage you to do the sacred work of embracing the parts of yourself you've been holding hostage or that have been holding you hostage. It's about releasing the emotional charge of judgment, integrating the places you've rejected, and uncovering the hidden gifts, talents, and powers they possess. It's about ending the war within. While it's good to understand the processes and the reasons behind them, we foremost want to understand how we can create real change. If you do the work—and don't just read about it—you will not be the same person when you finish this chapter. You will begin living a new story.

The Story of Your Life

Life doesn't happen to you. Life happens through you, through an activity of your consciousness. Put simply, everything is scripted in the mind—much of it unconsciously—and experience is just the projection of that inner movie. This means that outer conditions have no ultimate power over you. It may appear like they do; there seems to be all manner of forces aligned against or over us. But in the deepest mystical sense—even based on quantum physics—nothing outside of us has the final word on what we can do or who we can become. Take any challenge that seems like an insurmountable obstacle and you will find a story of someone who has proven its impotence in their life.

Except in moments of pure awakened awareness, you don't experience life directly. You experience your story or perception of life through these inner filters. You can be surrounded by opportunity, but if you're conditioned to see what's missing, that's *all* you'll see. Imagine a successful real estate developer and an angry activist walking down a New York street when they pass a dilapidated lot. The activist laments about this blemish on the block, decrying how bad the economy is and how low the city has sunk. The real estate developer exclaims what a perfect spot this is for a new high-rise hotel. A year later, the activist is still broke and fighting the system, while the real estate developer is breaking ground on a new hotel that will improve the system, creating dozens of jobs, adding tens of thousands in tax revenue to the city, and adding to his own bottom line.

Same situation, different consciousness.

Sometimes our outlook on life is based on a completely false judgment. One woman I knew, Jenn, struggled with self-worth issues most of her life and could never understand why or how to overcome them until she underwent hypnosis and recalled being abandoned in a shopping cart by her mother. On the surface, it appeared to be a non-event, but for this little girl it was a moment of pure terror as she looked around and realized she was alone. A moment later her mother returned, but the damage had been done. In that emotionally charged instance, Jenn made a powerful decision about herself, life, and her relationship to others: she wasn't worth sticking around for, she was on her own, and life was dangerous.

Try as she did to forgive her mother and heal this pain, she was unable to. But determined to move past this, she finally confronted her mother about this experience, only to learn that *her mother had never left her*. She had only stepped around the end of an aisle to grab something. From the child's vantage point, she couldn't see her mother. But from the mother's position, she never took her eyes off her daughter. The reality was that the mother had been there all along, but the story the child told herself—and then lived her life based on—was a fictional tale of being unloved, unwanted, and unsafe.

This is often how our life stories are woven. We have an experience and, with limited information, decide what it means—what life is, who others are, and who we are in relation to it all—and then create coping and defense mechanisms to survive the story we've created. Most, if not all, of the actual threats that caused us to create our story no longer exist in our life (except the ones we're perpetuating with our defense mechanisms). Yet we continue to live *as if they do*.

Not every moment has this story-creating power. But a handful of key events can cause us to make core decisions that shape the story of our life. For example, let's say you decide you have been rejected by a friend, a family member, or a lover and, scene by scene, you begin to play the part of a rejected person, looking for evidence of why you are unworthy, on guard for the next letdown. Events begin to build on themselves within the context of your story, reaffirming your unconscious commitments, until the cognitive dissonance will not allow you to see the good things that don't fit your story. Just as when you buy a new car or a new pair of shoes and start seeing similar ones everywhere, once you've identified with a certain story, evidence that supports it is all you see until it becomes self-perpetuating. As the saying goes, "If all you have is a hammer, everything looks like a nail." Likewise, if you're living a story of being a victim, everything and everyone looks like—and too often becomes—a potential victimizer.

This isn't to trivialize the traumas we face. Painful things happen; there's no denying that. But it's not the events that shape our character or future; it's how we interpret them—the decisions we make about ourselves, our relationship to others, and life in general. That's why two people can have the same experience and one becomes empowered while the other is emotionally crippled. But decisions we've made in the past don't have to be permanent. When we uncover them and decide to make new ones or gain a deeper understanding of the true meaning and purpose of the event, we actually change our past and begin to live like the person we could have been if things had worked out the way we wanted.

Even when we aren't able to uncover the inciting incident behind our present pain, we can still make a new choice and begin to tell a new story that is more congruent with the life we aspire to live, the life that is really in us. I recall the story of Paul, a man who believed he'd had a bad childhood and experienced all the limitations that go along with that belief—emotionally, creatively, and financially. Then one day, after another painful breakup reaffirmed how much he'd been screwed up, he had a moment of grace and decided to change his mind about his childhood. He began to affirm "I had a good childhood" and contemplate all the ways this was true.

On the surface, it seemed completely illogical. But soon new and better memories began to emerge: coming home from school and being served milk and cookies by his mom, sitting on his dad's lap and watching television, being read a bedtime story. Scene by scene, the evidence began to mount, persuading him that things weren't as bad as he'd long remembered. He wasn't denying the painful stuff, but he was no longer focusing on it. And as his story changed, his character changed. He grew confident, self-assured, and more creative and found a new level of ease and power. In other words, *he emerged as a man who'd had a good childhood.*

But there's a deeper dimension to reinterpreting our story. Not only are most circumstances not entirely what we perceive them to be but there's often a bigger purpose at play within them, the way every character and plot twist in a great story has been perfectly designed to illuminate the ultimate theme. And when you tap into the divine author's intent, not only can you turn a bad childhood into a good one—and reap the rewards of that new perspective— but you can also unlock a power in these key moments, which prepares you for the emergence of your soul's true purpose.

Rewriting Your Life Story

In the following process, you'll be guided back to a time when you had one of these core experiences and made a powerful decision that colored the rest of your life. Before this key moment, things were different. You didn't see life the way you do now. You had never felt the chronic emotion you now feel around this area. It may not have been the most traumatic event of your life. Sometimes a seemingly innocuous scene can create a new perception that builds into more powerful emotional moments. But we're not going to dwell on this past moment as it was. Instead, we're going to rise above it to discover the deeper purpose it holds. This will liberate you from a sense of victimhood and unlock untapped potential as you rewrite your history.

The exercise below is quite complex but very rewarding. You can read through it first and then do it from memory; you can have a friend or loved one guide you through it; or you can record yourself reading it and use that to guide you.

The Timeline Process

Get comfortable. Take a deep inhale, breathing light into your heart. As you exhale, release anything that no longer serves you, any excess or toxic energy. Gently become aware of an area where you feel stuck, where you feel a chronic emotion or where you know (or suspect) you've made a limiting decision.

Imagine that you begin to rise above your body, above your home, high in the air until you're floating above a time stream, or timeline, of your life that stretches from past to present and into the future. Feel free to visualize it as moving from left to right or back to front, whatever feels most natural to you. Float there for a moment.

Get in touch with that chronic emotion you've identified. Is it fear, anger, overwhelm, hopelessness? Where is it in your body? What's its color, shape, temperature? Notice what thoughts arise as you focus on this feeling. Are there any stories around it? You can also focus on your most painful limiting belief: "I'm unworthy. I'm ugly. I'm a failure." Or a belief specific to your stuck area: "I'll never amount to anything. I always have too much to do and too little time." If you're not sure what to work with, look at an area where you're struggling and notice what the common emotions or beliefs are. Imagine there's a dial beside you, and as you turn it up, allow the intensity of this emotion to increase. Give yourself permission to feel it fully.

In a moment, you're going to float back to the key event when you first had this feeling or created this belief. It may not have been the most intense experience, but it was the *first time* you had this emotion or made this decision. From that moment forward, you thought or felt it periodically, probably with growing intensity, until it became a part of your nervous system and habitual mental-emotional pattern.

Slowly begin to float back along your timeline. Don't force it. Trust your spirit; it knows what it's doing. Your innate wisdom is guiding, directing, and protecting this session. As you continue to float back, you begin to feel something pulling you. Like a homing beacon, this emotional pattern is taking you back to the place and time it was born. Trust that your subconscious mind knows right where it needs to go . . . all the way back to that moment when you first felt this emotion.

Drop down to that spot on the timeline and look around. Notice where you are, who you're with, how old you are, and what is happening, even if it's just flashes of memories, partial pictures. Whatever's coming up is perfectly fine. Your heart and soul know what to do. Just take note of how it feels, who is there, and what's happening.

Now rise back up out of that event, floating back to a moment before it ever happened, before you ever felt that negative emotion or made that limiting decision. Higher and higher until this event and your timeline are just a dot below and then gone completely from view. Far above your timeline, above this event, before it ever happened, this is your sacred space where you're deeply connected to your spirit, the part of you that knows that everything has a larger purpose.

You're open and ready to tap that divine wisdom, to remember the empowering reason you created this story for the evolution of your soul. It was created to make you dig deeper and reach higher, to open your heart, expand your mind, or awaken your spirit. There's some lesson of compassion or life theme you're meant to embody or model for others so you can deliver your gifts.

Whatever the powerful reason, you're about to discover it now.

Breathe and imagine that a colored light—whatever color you like— begins to pour down through the top of your head, filling you with the energy of this higher wisdom. As this sacred knowledge pours into your crown and fills your body, it strikes that mystic chord of memory, activating the divine DNA, that unique spiritual pattern of your being, reminding you who you really are, why you're really alive, and how this event was created to serve that purpose.

Listen as this deeper truth speaks to you. It might come in a word, an image, or a feeling. It might be flashes of memory, symbols, or sounds. Just pay attention to what comes. Take nothing for granted. Know and trust that the higher part of you, the divine author within, is speaking as this energy fills and renews you. Even if nothing seems to be coming, know that it is and that it's filling every part of your being. And as it does, all the false beliefs, negative emotions, and toxic energy of this limited perception are pushed out of every cell, out of every pore, appearing as smoke billowing out, floating off into space. Every atom is being cleansed of this negative charge and limiting belief. You're becoming purified, detoxified, as this truth fills every crevice of your consciousness.

Take a deep breath. Feel the shift happening. Feel this innate wisdom being integrated into you, readily accessible when you need it.

Let yourself float down toward the timeline again, pulsating with the color and the energy of this ancient truth. As you get closer, radiate it into the event, saturating everyone and everything with it. Drop into the event and look around, seeing everything shimmering with this energy and color. Notice how it feels now. Is the charge different?

Float back up, out of that event, feeling a new level of strength and intelligence being stored in your nervous system, reprogramming and realigning you, creating new neural pathways, changing you at a cellular and soul level—changing your history *and your future*. As you look forward on the timeline, you notice this new energy rippling forward from this event, shifting, redefining, and changing the color of the entire timeline. The size and shape of the timeline might even change as new tributaries and levels emerge.

As you begin to float forward along the timeline, any events connected to the initial one—where this old perception played out—pop up. As they do, blast them with the colored energy of this wisdom, saturating everyone and everything involved. Watch the events reintegrate into the timeline, creating more positive ripple effects all the way to the present and beyond. You continue to float forward, blessing and saturating every aspect of your timeline, until you reach the present moment.

You hover above it, taking a deep breath, letting this shift catch up to you, feeling that your history has changed. You're no longer the same character; you've got a bigger part in a bigger play now. All the wisdom you were meant to learn—the lessons, blessings, gifts, and energy—is now emerging, integrating within you.

You float forward on the timeline now, faster and faster as it zooms beneath you, all the way to one year from today. You hover above that date, looking back to today and beyond, seeing all the changes in your timeline, feeling all the inner shifts taking place from this newfound wisdom. Then you drop down into your timeline and look around.

Look at an area where you felt stuck. How is it now? Look in the mirror. Look at your relationships, your work, your finances. With your identity reclaimed and redeemed and this new energy and information cultivated, how has your life changed? What are you doing? Who are you doing it with and where? How are you feeling?

If any new issues are brought up, that's okay. In fact, it's good news. You're peeling away deeper unconscious layers ready to be healed. You can do this process on the new issue coming up or keep working on the old one until the charge is gone. No matter what's coming up, know that real work is being done, real change is taking place. Spirit is intangible; it's not audible, visible, or physical, so even when nothing appears to be happening, at a deeper level, something's working. You just may not know until it sprouts above the surface.

Allow yourself to be drawn back along the timeline, back to the present moment. Slowly drop down into your body, take a deep grounding breath, and feel gratitude for the work you've done.

When you're ready, open your eyes and take a few moments to journal about what came up. As you move through the rest of this day and week, pay attention to any dreams, emerging insights, emotions, or experiences. Likely they will be connected to the work you're doing. If your dreams take on a scary nature, don't worry; the ego views change as dangerous, so it can sometimes translate these inner transformations into what we call nightmares. Just keep doing the work, being kind and gentle with yourself. Whenever possible, seek support from others walking this path.

Growing Down: Embracing Your Shadow Side

Our darkness is potential light, and our shadow is the repressed dimension of our self. In truth, there's only wholeness. But as we travel along life's path and have core experiences, we make decisions about who we are and who we're not, and then we split our wholeness into two parts: our unconscious identity, which is the shadow, and our conscious identity, which is the mask. As we experience all the potential qualities of being, we decide *I'm not that, I am that, I'm not that, I am that* . . . until we've divided up the pile. The "I am" becomes our ego and the "I'm not" becomes our shadow.

For example, say you had a controlling parent. Because of the pain this caused, you decided that controlling is bad and that you'll never be controlling. Controlling then got repressed, rejected, and became part of your shadow. Then the "I am"—your ego or personality—had to take on a counter quality to compensate. This can be called your mask. In this case, maybe you wear the mask of the free spirit or laid-back type. So you grow up avoiding structure, rules, and boundaries and become freewheeling and easy-going. You avoid commitments and confrontation—anything that might feel controlling to you or someone else. But this duality is not authentic; it's a coping mechanism to avoid the fear or shame this

quality is charged with and the perceived consequences of expressing it.

There are several problems with this. The first is that the duality,
the inauthenticity, is a form of resistance to the unresolved energy
within you. And that energy must find expression, whether it breaks
out as a sudden irrational need to seize control in a destructive
way, is reflected back as people trying to control you, or becomes
a compulsive need to avoid control at all costs, resulting in a major
crisis. In general it will lead to a life with unstable structure or no
structure at all—checkbooks that aren't balanced, plans that aren't
made or followed through on, money problems, commitment problems, problems with authority, and so on. In some cases we find
ourselves unable to control our desire to not be controlling (or
whatever quality we're battling with) and we become the thing we
hate most. Or the quality can also be internalized, where we control
ourselves in debilitating ways, parenting our inner child the way we
were parented.

Controlling is just one example. The destructive nature of the
shadow can be seen in many ways. It's the preacher who condemns
gays and then gets caught in a scandal with a gay lover; the politician who vehemently fights for family values and then gets caught
in an affair, has a child out of wedlock, or has multiple divorces. We
internalize the shadow, project it onto others, and then try to fix
them. Anytime someone's buttons are pushed, it's a sure sign of a
shadow. The one protesting the strongest is fighting their shadow
the hardest. And it's only a matter of time before the beast breaks
out and wreaks havoc.

For most of us, the sabotage takes on a less tabloid-worthy form.
We procrastinate, we don't communicate, we isolate, we eat, drink,
or shop too much, we get addicted or distracted, or we become self-
help junkies to try and get rid of all these bad parts. Eventually we
get stuck and end up in a rut, with no idea how we got there or how

to get out. And the last thing we think we need is to embrace the very parts of us we've spent a lifetime—and often a fortune—trying to run from, hide from, heal, fix, or eliminate.

But loving, accepting, and integrating these shadow parts is the only way to become free of their seemingly destructive nature. I say "seemingly" because there's nothing inherently negative about them; they're dimensions of our being that have been misjudged, misperceived, and misunderstood—and all their acting out is, as the familiar saying goes, a cry for love. They need our attention. They need their story to be heard, their pain to be felt, and to be accepted without any attempt to change them. Then they stop sabotaging us. The most profound part of this work is the realization that evil is just a part of life we're perceiving through a distorted lens of judgment and rejection—like looking in a funhouse mirror. The very word itself is "live" spelled backward.

You can't heal life by repressing it, you can't have more life by rejecting it, and you can't live more fully if you're at war with it. The path to healing any form of evil or negativity—inside or out—is by embracing it, seeing through the appearance to its true nature, and reintegrating its power. That's why all great masters have taught us to "love our enemy" and, even more to the point, that the so-called enemy is "within your own household," which, metaphysically speaking, refers to our mind or consciousness.

Taking Shadow Inventory

Let's discover what shadows are unconsciously operating in your life. To start, look at an area where you're struggling or feeling that emerging impulse to expand and be/do/have more. If it's an area of struggle, identify a part of this situation you have strong negative feelings around. Maybe it's an illness or financial problem that brings up strong emotions. Maybe you feel out of control, despairing, angry. Notice the feelings. Then ask yourself what you believe this means about you—the fact that you're out of work, overweight, broke, or just broken. Do you feel like a failure? What's the inner self-talk around this area? Do you call yourself lazy, stupid, worthless?

Become aware of these judgments without engaging them. Write them down. As you look at the situation you're struggling with, ask, "How would I or my life be better, different, or improved if I could overcome or achieve this?" Become aware of what arises; it may be a flash of memory, a feeling, a fleeting thought, or a clear inner voice. If no response comes, you can repeat the question again and let it roll around in your awareness. Regardless of what you receive, next ask, "What will I be if I don't change this or achieve my goal?" Notice any judgment that comes up, but don't engage in it. Remain a witness and take note of whatever arises.

Let's look at it from one more angle. Ask, "If I do this, achieve this, heal this, move beyond this, what am I afraid others will think about me?" For example, maybe you need to take better care of yourself, start exercising, meditating, taking time off . . . but you're afraid that people will think you're selfish or self-indulgent. Or you need to invest in yourself, which would mean not spending as much on others, but you're afraid that people will think you're stingy or greedy. Maybe you need to stand up, speak out, and confront someone, but you're afraid they'll think you're aggressive, mean, or an angry bitch! Perhaps you want to become a speaker, start a business, or do some other activity that would put you in front of people in a bigger way, but you're afraid they'll think you're arrogant, a show-off, a know-it-all, and just who the hell do you think you are, anyway?

Notice the strong feelings you have about staying stuck and the strong feelings about becoming free. Both carry a shadow. Write these insights down. Then look over what you've written. As you scan the qualities, which one has the strongest charge? Which one do you feel the most fear, shame, anger, or sadness around? Which one would you rather die than admit to? Is it the shame of being unworthy, unlovable, ugly, broken, or broke, or the fear of being judged as selfish, arrogant, angry, or controlling? Pay particular attention to the qualities you're *sure* you're not. If "thou dost protest too much," then "thou" most likely has a shadow around that area of protestation.

Once you identify a shadow that has the strongest charge, contemplate all the ways you've tried to deny, reject, fix, heal, or repress it. Become aware of how much energy you've expended trying to *not* be it. You've worked hard to hold it together, and to support this you've created a mask. If you have pain around being a "bad boy/ girl," you probably created the "good boy/girl" mask at great cost to your self-respect and fulfillment. If you have shame or fear around being selfish, you probably created the selfless or people-pleaser mask, saying yes to others when you mean no, saying no to yourself when you want to say yes—full of anger or resentment. Whatever these words and phrases bring up for you is revealing your unconscious projection or shadow around them.

It's been exhausting, hasn't it—all the masks, the manipulation, the unconscious agendas? And it hasn't really worked. If you have identified within you the shadow of being bad or unworthy and have taken on the mask of a people pleaser, you've probably noticed by now that no matter how much you try to please people, you never can. If you have the shadow of being a loser or being stupid and you counteract that by wearing the mask of the overachiever, you've probably wised up to the fact that no matter how much you achieve or how many letters you have behind your name, you still fear failure, or you feel like a failure and are afraid of being found out.

That doesn't mean you haven't developed some great qualities. A people pleaser develops real skill in connecting with others. A control freak develops real talent for structure and order. The overachiever achieves all kinds of things and grows in many ways. *These are the gifts of the shadow*, which you'll get a chance to discover more in the following process. But at a certain point, it's not enough; it doesn't work anymore, at least not as well as it used to. You're out of balance. Because you've developed your behavior in reaction to a false belief about yourself, you've only grown one dimension of yourself. You start to feel burned out and depressed, and you begin to sabotage your success. Or it's never worked and you've been trying to dig yourself out of a hole most of your life—and all the digging has only made the hole deeper.

We're going to work with these patterns now, not to destroy or get rid of them but to reconcile, reintegrate, and redeem them; we're going to take the energy you've been using to battle these enemies and turn them into allies—freeing the captive gifts, talents, and insights that have been locked up inside. That selfish part of you will become the master of self-care. The controlling self will create structures that support your ongoing growth. The bad kid will open up your wild, spontaneous side, allowing you to break the rules that have hobbled you and make you an innovative—if sometimes rebellious—leader in your own right. The angry self will teach you about real boundaries and inner authority. And the unworthy self will make you humble and receptive enough to receive divine guidance and support.

Imagine no longer battling yourself. Imagine genuinely loving and accepting *all of you*. Not only will you finally feel at home in your own heart but you'll also have a depth of compassion, understanding, and healing influence for everyone around you.

Entering the House of Shadows: A Meditation

Look back at your list of shadow qualities and decide which one to focus on first. This is who you'll meet in your inner shadow estate. You can read through this exercise and then do it from memory, have a friend read it and guide you, or record it so that you can play it back to yourself. Once you become familiar with the process, you can adapt it according to your needs.

Get into a comfortable position. Close your eyes and take a nice deep breath into your heart. Exhale anything that no longer serves you. Repeat this a few times, relaxing into this moment.

In your mind's eye, imagine you're standing before a mysterious forest with towering trees. You begin to walk along a path, feeling the mists of this ancient place as you enter into it. With every step, you feel the normal world fading away and the inner world of enchantment growing thicker around you. Deeper and deeper you walk into the forest, until nothing of the old world remains. It's not threatening at all; it has a magical quality, a sense of adventure and possibility.

In a clearing ahead, you see a magnificent estate that blends into the lush surroundings. Picture it however you feel best represents your inner mansion, the place where the characters of your unconscious dwell. You follow a path over a small bridge that crosses a body of water surrounding your mansion and make your way to the large double doors of the entrance.

With a gentle push, the doors swing open. You take a moment to look around your mansion's foyer, noticing the décor, and then turn to the right and head down a long corridor with doors on either side. You begin to walk down this hall, passing closed rooms, feeling yourself going deeper into this inner estate, into areas that haven't been visited for a long time—maybe never—rooms that house the artifacts and archetypes that make up the stories of your life.

This is where your shadows live. You feel yourself drawn to a particular door. This is the room where the specific shadow you've chosen resides.

You open the door and step inside, finding yourself in the environment of this shadow. What do you see? Are you indoors? Outdoors? Is the setting tropical, forest, or desert? You step in and look around, feeling the floor or ground beneath your feet, noticing the ceiling or sky above. You feel the temperature against your skin and hear the sounds of other elements or creatures that inhabit this place.

You make your way to your meditation spot—a chair, a couch, a tree stump, the grass, whatever is comfortable—and invite this shadow quality to join you. Notice where it comes from in this environment, and as it approaches, be aware of how it's dressed, how it moves, how it holds itself.

Take a deep breath and begin the inquiry, asking this shadow when it first came into your life or when you first rejected it. What was that event or moment that caused you to judge, deny, or repress it? The shadow might describe it or you might find an image presenting itself in your mind's eye. It may be vivid and concrete or just brief flashes, thoughts, or feelings. Take nothing for granted. Give yourself time to allow the event to coalesce if it feels like there's more there to be seen or experienced.

Ask this shadow one or more of these questions: "How have you served me since this event? Why did you show up in my life? How have you been my ally instead of my enemy? What are you here to teach me? How have you been helping me grow all along?" For example, if it's the lazy shadow, created because your father used to shame or punish you for hanging out, sleeping in, or not doing your chores, and you decided you would never be lazy, maybe your rejection of this shadow caused you to become hard-working and productive, and as a result you've created some real success in your life.

Now ask, "What is the blessing or lesson you bring me? What do you need to tell me or teach me now? What is your beneficial purpose in my life presently?" This helps you see the positive spin on what seemed like a destructive quality. For example, because you rejected your lazy self (or whatever shadow you're working with), you don't allow yourself to rest. As a result, you're a stressed-out workaholic, you don't spend enough time with loved ones, and you don't have much fun because when you're not working hard, you feel the fear/ shame/guilt of this lazy shadow. So maybe the positive expression of this quality is not about being lazy but about taking time off, resting, playing, finding better balance and renewal, which will ultimately make you even more productive.

This next question is one of the most important. Ask, "What do you need from me to feel loved and accepted so you can take your right-ful, constructive place in my life?" You're not asking what it needs from you to change from being lazy to productive, sad to happy, or controlling to carefree; you're asking what the shadow needs in order to feel loved and accepted *as it is*. You've been judging this part as bad and trying to repress, reject, or change it, and that has caused it to act out in order to get your attention—like a child crying out.

What this part needs most is to be seen, heard, and unconditionally loved. Ask it what it needs from you to feel respected, validated, and appreciated. As you get guidance, make sure it's specific and action-able. Things like "love yourself more" or "speak your truth" are not guidance yet. Dig deeper: "How should I love myself more? What would it look like to love myself more? Where should I speak my truth? What should I say?"

The lazy shadow might say things like, "I need you to take a break, start meditating, rest when you're tired, take the week-ends off, exercise and take better care of yourself, take a walk on the beach or in the woods, relax, smell the flowers . . ." If it's the greedy shadow, she might say, "I need you to stop buying expensive gifts for everyone, stop spending money you don't have, keep more of the money you make and put it in savings or invest it." Or if it's the controlling shadow, he might say, "I need you to create more structure in your life, like a yearly plan, weekly agenda, and daily routines. I need you to create better boundaries for your kids, who are acting out because they're given too much space. Give them clear bedtimes and television and computer limits—and stick to them no matter what."

If the guidance brings up resistance, this is the emotional pattern of the shadow. If you need to create boundaries for your kids, you might fear that they'll think you're a mean parent. This could spark a memory of how controlling *your* parents were, how bad it made you feel, and how you made the decision to never be like that. This is good. It's shaking things loose, bringing them to the surface to be embraced and integrated. Breathe and listen. If you need more rein-forcement, ask, "What will my life be like if I follow the guidance and integrate this shadow? What new powers and abilities will it bring me? How will I look and feel? How will things be better?"

Thank this part of you for sharing, no matter what came up. Ask it to forgive you for any way you've abused it. See and feel the shadow give you its forgiveness. Embrace it and tell it you'll never abandon it again; you'll always be here for it. As you hold the shadow, notice how it evolves or changes. Maybe it's not quite the bedraggled, weak, or scary-looking character anymore. It's been redeemed. *And then it merges with you, becoming one.* Take a deep breath as you feel this part of you becoming integrated within.

Feel grateful for the deep work you've done and then make your way back out the door, down this corridor, and into the foyer. Take a deep breath, feeling the satisfaction of a job well done, and then exit through the large front door. Make your way over the bridge, onto the path, glancing back at your mansion with gratitude for the deep work that has gone on inside. Then head back into the forest and out the other side, into the light of the "ordinary world." Pause to feel the new energies and insights stirring within you. Something has shifted. You're not the same person who entered that enchanted forest; you're more yourself, more alive.

When you're ready, open your eyes. Take time to journal. Drink some water. Take a hot bath or a nice walk. And pay attention as the days go by. Notice how you respond to people and how they respond to you. Perhaps you'll discover that you're no longer bothered by a quality in other people that used to push your buttons, or at least not at the same level. Maybe you'll see your projections more clearly and more easily take responsibility for your reactions, which is the beginning of true freedom, of really owning your life. For more in-depth shadow work, explore Debbie Ford's *Dark Side of the Light Chasers*[7] or the collected works of C. G. Jung.

You're now on the path to embracing everything that seems broken, embracing it all in the light of wholeness, creating this primary condition for your greatest Emergence. This is the beginning of a beautiful friendship with yourself.

The Healing Heart

There are two key takeaways here: (1) you don't have to fix yourself; you have to embrace, integrate, and redeem the parts you've judged and rejected; and (2) you must build this into a way of life, not a one-off practice. This isn't something you do a couple of times and you're done, any more than having a couple of conversations with an estranged family member will heal that relationship and allow it to thrive. That would be crazy, right? But that's how we often treat ourselves. We do a weekend workshop on self-love, get in touch with our inner child, and then get angry when that child acts up the following week and start beating him up again.

Remember, these shadows are like children you've abandoned, disowned, judged, or criticized—probably for years. But the fact is that for a long time, you've believed the way to heal, grow, and improve is to judge, shame, or beat the bad parts out of yourself. And now you're holding an intervention of sorts, a family reunion, bringing together these seemingly broken and divided members to learn how to love each other again. That takes time. It's certainly possible to experience radical breakthroughs—just as you can have a major healing of a relationship by finally getting honest and forgiving. But more often it's a gradual process of regaining the trust of these aspects of yourself, rebuilding rapport, getting to know who they really are, what they really care about and want, and how to meet their needs.

It's probably not necessary to sit down every day and do the shadow work or timeline process, but it's not a bad idea to do it once or twice a week to start. As you get more familiar with a shadow, you can check in more informally throughout the day or week. And when you feel particularly out of sorts (angry, sad, scared), you can embrace or soothe that part of yourself like you would an upset child, rather than resort to a knee-jerk response of trying to shut them up, ignore them, or eat/drink/shop/work over these feelings. Imagine you have a sign above you that says *All feelings welcome*. And begin to practice relaxing into the feelings as they arise instead of resisting them. The more you make *all of yourself welcome*, the less noise these parts will make to get your attention.

Loving these parts of yourself doesn't mean you let them control you. You're still the boss. It's like having an upset child trying to get your attention while you're in the middle of an important phone call. As a parent, you wouldn't necessarily drop everything. You might put them on your lap and comfort them while you continue your call. But sometimes you have to be firmer. If they're having a tantrum and not respecting your space, you might have to tell them in a loving but strong voice that they're not allowed to act out and you'll attend to them *after* you finish whatever you're working on. If you're consistent with this, you create boundaries that make the child feel *more* secure and cause them to act out less.

The same is true with aspects of yourself. You can't just melt down every time one of these parts of you freaks out. Nor can you always stop and meditate. And as you build this position of authority, like a strong, loving parent, these parts of you will get the message. They'll become more secure in you and you'll become more emotionally stable.

As you practice this, just remember the cardinal rule:

You're not doing this to change these parts of you.

When we begin this work, it's common for the ego to take over again. We think we're doing the shadow work to love these parts of ourselves, but it's often the ego trying to manipulate them into doing what we want. We're not listening and embracing because we love them for who and what they are; we're doing it so they'll stop acting out, start being happy, and help us accomplish what we want in the world. This doesn't work. It's like trying to build a relationship with a child who is acting out. We sit down and ask how they're doing, what they're feeling, and what they need from us. It looks like the right actions. But we have an agenda: get them happy and in line so they'll take out the trash. And they know it, if only unconsciously. They sense the manipulation and they won't open up. Or if they do, and we hit them with a demand or request, they close right back up. The trust takes a dive, and it takes even longer to rebuild it.

These inner parts of you know when your intentions are sincere and unconditional. They know if you really care or if you're just trying to whip them into shape so they'll get back to doing your bidding. So check your intentions when you begin and remind yourself of your true purpose. Seek nothing from these parts of you except understanding. Have no desire but to unconditionally love and accept them. They deserve it. They're worthy of your love.

They are, after all, you.

This is a journey into the heart of God. It seeks nothing. It loves because loving is its nature. It sees nothing but itself, the image and likeness of the divine. Ultimately, this practice of healing ourselves is about awakening our healing heart—our Christ-like or Buddha-like nature. That, finally, is the *real* reason we created this divine drama: to awaken to the truest, deepest meaning and measure of love.

Welcome home to your wholeness.

STAGE SEVEN

WAIT ON THE LAW

Infinite patience produces immediate results.
FROM *A COURSE IN MIRACLES*

The Chinese bamboo tree is one of the greatest teachers of patience. You plant the bamboo rhizome—like a piece of ginger root shoots and roots will sprout from—water it, feed it, and, for the next four or five years, you see pretty much no change at all. To all appearances, nothing productive is happening. If you're inclined toward get-rich-quick opportunities or are a results-driven person, you might be driven mad or at least driven away.

But if you can withstand the waiting, if you can continue cultivating the soil regardless of the lack of short-term rewards, you will be rewarded greatly. In the fifth year, the bamboo springs to life and grows up to eight stories tall in six weeks. Guinness World Records attributes the fastest growing plant to certain species of bamboo, which have been found to grow up to thirty-five inches per day.[1] During those years of apparent dormancy, beneath the surface where very little stirs, a strong root system develops, deep and broad enough to not only hold up that eighty-plus-foot stalk but also to draw from the soil all the rich nutrients needed for such growth.

The Three Faces of Waiting

In this age of quick-fix microwave mind-sets, most of us want what we want, and we want it now—whether it's instant download speed, lottery riches, or the next version of the iPhone. But just as you can't force the bamboo to grow before it has established a system that can support it, you can't force your seed of potential to grow until it's ripe and ready. If you build it *inside*, they will come *outside*, but you can't control the timeline, since you don't always know what's being built.

Waiting is part of the perfect process.

I don't mean waiting in a passive sense, sitting around watching paint dry. On the path of Emergence, waiting is an active experience that requires courage and strength of character. But waiting has different levels. On one level, it *is* stopping and doing nothing when everything in us wants to do something—*anything*—to get what we think we need. This takes increasing faith and inner resolve. On another level, waiting is having an inner stillness and receptivity to what's unfolding. On the surface of our daily life, we appear to be doing nothing or very little, but inside we are developing our soul-senses to see, hear, and receive the guidance and nourishment we truly need to thrive long-term. And finally, waiting is about staying planted where we are, growing down, our roots running deep enough to contact the *true source of our fulfillment* so we can withstand the barren times and inevitable storms and bear fruit richly in our season.

The emerging impulse has a purpose for you. And with this purpose comes a message, a medium, and a mission. But without a strong inner foundation, you can be swayed by outer conditions, trends, and the winds of public opinion. The goal is to become so deeply rooted in the soil of your soul that you are nourished by the silent stream of life running beneath the surface—a source that is neither determined nor diminished by outer circumstances—and rise taller and stronger than ever before.

To develop healthy roots, we must understand our thresholds of consciousness—the boundaries of our self-concept that determine what we believe is possible and shape our identity. When we begin to grow and bump up against these boundaries, we trigger coping and defense mechanisms designed to keep us the same. It's an evolutionary artifact that helped our species survive by ensuring that we didn't explore too far beyond the familiar borders, where we might get lost, get eaten, or starve. But this survival mechanism often hinders our growth now. These thresholds prevent us from breaking new ground and going deeper, keeping us in our familiar patterns. The result is that the average person doesn't live seventy to ninety years; they live the same year seventy to ninety times!

Ultimately, the primary purpose of Emergineering is to generate the inner conditions that are congruent with your highest vision, allowing you to feel fulfilled and successful even when outer conditions don't yet reflect it. It's learning to be *in* the world but not *of* it, less attached to outcome and more attuned to outgo, the natural radiance of your being. When you can achieve this, which this chapter aims to help you do, it leads to "the infinite patience that produces immediate results"[2] and, ultimately, to true freedom.

Your Field of Dreams

There's a story of Ali Hafed, an ancient Persian man who lived near the river Indus and owned a large farm and orchard. He was content with his life, albeit not one inspired by a vision. One day a Buddhist priest shared with him a parable about how the world was made, particularly how diamonds came to be—as "congealed drops of sunlight"—and their immense value. "One diamond the size of your thumb could buy you the entire county," the priest said. Ali was so moved by this vision of wealth that he decided that he would find his own diamond mine and asked the priest where these diamonds were buried. The priest described a river that runs between high mountains and through white sands and said that Ali would find his diamonds in those sands. Ali doubted that these precious stones existed or were accessible to him. He didn't know of any such place as the priest described, and he didn't know where to start. But the priest insisted that all he had to do was "go and find them."

Driven by the ambition of his vision, Ali sold everything he had to fund his journey, left his family in his neighbor's care, and set out searching for these proverbial gems in mountains, rivers, and sands, from Palestine to Europe to Spain, never staying long, impatient with lust for this treasure, haunted by the lingering doubts of whether it even existed and if he could ever find it. Finally, he found himself broke, suffering, and dying on the shore of a bay in Barcelona, where the great waves rolled in between the Pillars of Hercules. And having lost all hope and vision, he cast himself into the violent waters and sank beneath the foam, never again to be seen.

Some time later, the man who bought Ali's farm brought his camel into the garden to drink from the stream that ran through the white sands. And there, gleaming in the sunlight, he found a stone shimmering with a many-colored hue. He put it upon his mantel and thought nothing of it until the Buddhist priest visited one day and, seeing the glint of light on the mantel, realized that Ali's successor had found a diamond. But not only a single diamond; when they returned to the garden and dug up the sands, they discovered handfuls of these precious gems, each one even more magnificent than the last. This would later become known as the diamond mine of Golconda, the richest diamond mine in history, one that would eventually bring forth the crown jewels of England and Russia and even the Hope Diamond.

Had Ali remained at home, or at least returned home and dug into his own field, instead of searching far and wide in strange lands, driven by both fear and ambition until he was driven to death—he would have found "acres of diamonds" in his own backyard.[3]

How Deep Are You Willing to Dig?

One key distinction that separates achievers from nonachievers is that nonachievers give up when things get hard and results aren't forthcoming, whereas achievers keep going, no matter what, until they reach their goal. Although Ali *did* struggle against all odds, many of those obstacles were self-created, and in the end he gave up. But another equally important distinction of the greatest achievers, those who endure and grow stronger from their pursuits rather than being broken by them, is that they know *they* are their greatest resource, that within *them*—in their own backyard—is where the real treasure is buried.

We're all given a field of dreams, rich with potential, but what we do with it determines what we bring forth. Like Ali, many hopeful treasure hunters don't even think to start digging where they live. And for others, whether they begin at home or elsewhere, they rarely dig long enough to strike that rich ore beneath the surface. Driven by their vision of possibility, they stake their claim, start digging, and find a few flecks of gold. But soon they hit bedrock, experience difficulties with little or no rewards, and give up. They get impatient, frustrated, and bored. They think something's wrong with them, the tools, or the location. They lose faith in the spot they've picked, buy better tools, and find another spot—only to have the story repeat itself again and again. And at the end of their life, they have a field of half-dug holes and broken dreams.

The person who ultimately succeeds is no different than the person who does not, save for one key difference: the achiever refuses to give up. Both experience the same things—the burst of hope and enthusiasm (the field of possibilities, the flecks of gold), followed by challenges that cause doubt, discouragement, disappointment, and disillusionment. They wonder if it's the right spot, the right tools—or if they're right in the head!

But achievers keep digging anyway—in *their own* field, not someone else's.

They stick with it until they break through the bedrock and bring forth a bounty of results. Then they build a structure around it (rituals, plans, accountability, deep habits) so that it becomes sustainable. They're not just in it for the quick fix; they're in it to build a real business, a lifelong practice, a fully developed product, or a deeply engaged relationship—whatever their big vision is.

Crossing the Thresholds

As we've touched on before, the obstacles you face trigger these inner thresholds and are, in a very real sense, a reflection of them. They're part of the ego's survival system, designed to protect and preserve you. To the ego, the emotional pain of being pushed past the boundaries of our known self is a sign of danger—and real transformation is equivalent to death. This system once served us. Long ago, if we left the cave at the wrong time, moved somewhere new, or wandered off the beaten path, we could have frozen to death, starved to death, or been eaten by a saber-toothed cat. The ego structure maintained our sense of separation from all the dangers (animals, enemies, the elements), keeping us in self-preservation mode.

Whereas earlier in our evolution, significant change could have meant our demise, now it's the opposite: not changing or evolving could end our species. When we hit these thresholds of consciousness, we must recognize what's really happening and override it. Waiting on the Law means trusting that the seeds you're planting *are* growing and staying the course in the face of most evidence to the contrary. The challenge is that this coping mechanism has had a long time to develop. It's clever at convincing us we can't change or tricking us into believing we *are* changing when all we're doing is moving from one spot on the field to the next, never getting much beneath the surface, where our richest resources are buried. Our ego knows our fears and fantasies and uses that insider information to manipulate us into choosing validation over vision, comfort over commitment, or security over self-actualization.

The frustration, doubt, blame, or impatience we experience with the Emergence process are all directly attributable to this long-entrenched function of the ego. And if that's not enough, the ego strikes closer to home. You know the familiar refrain: "I'm too old, I'm too young; I'm too fat, I'm too thin; I don't have enough money, I don't have enough time, I don't have enough support, and I don't have enough knowledge—basically, I suck!" Sometimes there's even evidence to back this up—oh, how the ego loves having evidence to make its case! You might really feel tired. You might actually not have the cash to invest in that program. You might be facing serious obstacles. And if you accept the ego's closing argument, which says that this is all evidence of why you can't make it, you'll lose.

Over the past two decades, I've worked with many people who didn't believe they had the time, support, or money to move forward. All inner and outer evidence told them to give up and stop believing in their miracle. I've personally hit the thresholds more times than I can remember and even lived inside them for long stretches, traversing the length of those trenches beneath the border walls that separated who I was from who I could become. Part of what kept me going was blind ambition, gullibility, and ignorance of the facts. When that ran its course, panic and desperation kicked in. I've watched this pattern repeat itself with my clients, with an almost predictable regularity. And in nearly every case, it was having a clear, compelling vision, rooted in their core values, and a practice anchored in these principles that gave them the courage and capacity to march on. Instead of trying to avoid the thresholds, it became about digging into them, digging under the walls, and coming out the other side. This not only created the breakthroughs they yearned for but the process made them strong enough to handle the next leg of the journey.

Remember, whatever's missing is what you're not giving. This applies as much to the little but still important things as it does to the big life-changing ones. As I described previously, there are many times when my clients are tired and don't want to exercise, but when they follow this practice and do it anyway, the energy follows. On a weekly basis, I coach people who don't feel inspired to do the work required to achieve their dreams, but because they've committed to their vision, they do it—and inspiration follows. Or it doesn't. But they write those pages, paint those pictures, or develop that business plan anyway.

They've built a habit.

The same is true with spiritual practice. Many days, even months, can go by where your spiritual work doesn't seem to bear much fruit. It would be easy to change practices, doubt your faith, or give up altogether. But in all my encounters with spiritual masters, my own clients, and myself, it's during these periods where we must plant ourselves in our meditation chair and dig our roots into the soil of our soul that the deepest, most lasting work is done, although the results may not be evident for months or years to come. As Samuel Johnson said, "The chains of habit are too weak to be felt until they are too strong to be broken."[4]

Anyone who thrives in any endeavor develops this discipline, the ability to be still, to stay the course, to grow down—*no matter what*. No matter how the world receives them. No matter what results they get initially. Reportedly, a poem that hung on Mother Teresa's Calcutta home, summed up this attitude beautifully:

People are often unreasonable, irrational, and self-centered,
Love, them anyway.

If you do good, people will accuse you of selfish,
   ulterior motives,
Do good anyway.
If you are successful, you will win false friends
   and true enemies,
Succeed anyway.
The good you do will be forgotten tomorrow,
Do good anyway.
Honesty and frankness make you vulnerable,
Be honest and frank anyway.
What you spend years building may be destroyed
   overnight,
Build anyway.
If you find serenity and happiness, some may be jealous,
Be happy anyway.
Give the world the best you have and you'll get kicked
   in the teeth,
Give the world the best you've got anyway.[5]

This is even more meaningful now that we know that Mother Teresa suffered from a crisis of faith for many years, struggling to cross this threshold. But because of her practice and commitment, *she did it anyway*. Thresholds are part of life. You're going to hit them. You won't get what you want all the time, you won't feel like doing what must be done, the world will misunderstand and reject you, and there will be dark nights of the soul. Things *will* break down.

But if you understand and practice this principle, you'll break through these thresholds, out of these loops of limited identity, and have real growth and progress. Make the commitment to your vision and stay the course. And when the thresholds tempt you to believe you can't go on, *do it anyway*.

Get Your Gift before You Go

The modus operandi of the average human being is to try to improve their circumstances and, at the same time, avoid change. This seems understandable at first. But because such a static existence rarely leads to lasting peace or fulfillment, we're left wanting, living lives of quiet desperation and dissatisfaction. True joy and meaning can only come from the development of our deeper potential. You can't change your circumstances and remain the same any more than an acorn can stay an acorn *and* become an oak tree. Improving our lives requires that we stop seeking merely a better human experience and, like Jacob from the Old Testament, wrestle our angels until they yield their blessings of transformation.

Whether our struggle is that we're trapped in an irreconcilable relationship, an unredeemable job, or an intractable physical ailment, none of us can escape this stage. The knee-jerk response is to want to get out of it, get rid of it, or find something better—to flee in the middle of the night and wake up where nobody knows our name or game. But we can't leave our troubles behind; they're an expression of our consciousness. So we perpetuate and exacerbate our suffering and prolong the time when we'll have to get in the ring with God and make that connection our soul is longing for—the thing that will bring us the life we truly desire.

One sure sign that we have work to do, whether in a relationship, a job, or any situation we want to get out of, is our emotional reaction to it. If it's still pushing our buttons, it's about us, not the people we're reacting to. That doesn't mean they don't have a part in it; it just means we're shadow dancing with them, projecting our unresolved issues onto them. They're just a proxy to fix our projection on. It also doesn't mean you should always stay where you are, especially if it's destructive or physically harmful. If you find yourself in a situation where you are experiencing abuse, *get out immediately* and work with these principles from a distance. But often when we "feel" abused, we're just caught in a war with ourselves, experiencing the internalized and unresolved trauma of our childhood. It's important for your health, safety, and well-being to make this distinction.

For example, a colleague or loved one says something to us that seems critical or uncaring or they try to control our every move around a particular subject and we find ourselves thinking that this is abusive behavior. If we've truly done everything we can in terms of owning our reaction, acknowledging our role in the altercation, and, if necessary, taking an empowered stand for what feels right and they still don't change their behavior, then it very well might be abusive. At the very least, it might become clear that it's not a relationship that respects and values us, and from our newly empowered position, we may choose to move on. In any case, if we want to heal the situation once and for all, we must make a distinction: Are the emotions of pain and suffering coming from what we're *thinking, feeling, and projecting* onto the person or situation? Or are they coming from the actual conditions of the situation? If we react to that projection, blame the appearance, and leave, we'll just project it all over again.

New setting, same story.

What's worse, it can take weeks, months, or even years to build back up to the place where we're shadow dancing again, so the realization may dawn on us only gradually that we are back in the same situation, and the sense of lost time and regret is multiplied. So if you're already in the heat of a powerful projection—a job or relationship where you're feeling strong negative emotions—*take advantage of that*. Don't run away in the dark of night; stay with the shadow and do the work! This is fertile soil for growth. Don't waste the hard work you've put in and fall into the trap of believing the next relationship, job, or project is going to save you. It never will. The salvation you're seeking *is within you, in this moment.*

If you're in a relationship and you're bored, angry, or feeling like your partner is not meeting your needs, or you've fallen out of love, leaving won't necessarily make you feel more seen, heard, or valued. If you're in a job where you feel disrespected, invalidated, or unappreciated, quitting won't automatically make you feel the validation and approval you seek. You might get a short-term high from venting your feelings and reacting to what Eckhart Tolle calls your "pain-body," which is an accumulation of old emotional pain that acts like an entity and feeds off negative emotions to survive.[6] But it won't last. Soon you'll be face-to-face with yourself again, feeling all the same feelings, only now you won't have anyone to blame them on and these feelings will turn on you.

Remember, your real goal is not to manipulate and control outer appearances until they make you feel better; it's to align with your inner essence that already feels great. Then outer circumstances will shape themselves around that. This sometimes requires you to be patient and work through these layers. You must see past the lies you've unwittingly bought into, feel the emotions you've buried, integrate the shadows you've rejected, and finally lay claim to the truth of your being. That's your threshold moment, maybe even a threshold year. It's an evolutionary turning point, designed by your soul to take you deeper, make you stronger, and activate latent powers and potentials within you, a divinity that would not otherwise be stirred into activity. When you frame it this way, you realize that your opponent—whether it's a boss, a mate, a family member, or a condition—is your greatest teacher, your guru, the divine itself appearing to help you take your life to the next level.

This is a difficult teaching, and that may be why so few follow it. The honeymoon period of a new job or new relationship feels wonderful. All those endorphins and pheromones—everything is beautiful and possible again! But it's a trick of the ego to keep you the same while convincing you you're changing. If no real inner change has happened—if the story hasn't fundamentally changed through a more integrated, expanded awareness of your true nature, you'll soon be back in the same play with a new cast of characters. As I described in the beginning of this book, you might get a bigger paycheck but you'll end up broke at a higher income bracket. You might get a new job but have the same jerky boss in a different uniform. You might even get a new mate but end up in the same arguments because the fight was always with yourself.

But the real tragedy is that you not only end up dealing with many of the same issues over and over or repressing them and shutting down more parts of your self, but you never get to experience, express, and share your true purpose—the deepest, richest, juiciest parts of yourself. You're like a character stuck in Act One of your play, and the real adventure doesn't start until Act Two. The genius potential, the ecstasy and bliss, your true destiny of greatness—whether in work, relationships, creativity, or spiritual discovery—is beyond the threshold.

Let's cross that threshold together.

Mapping the Thresholds

Take a moment to reflect over the last year—or the last few—and see if you notice a pattern. Are you one of those individuals who jumps from relationship to relationship, job to job, project to project but doesn't experience a sense of completion or fulfillment? Perhaps the pattern is to break things off just before you get into a real relationship, give up just before you go for the job you really want, or get bored, scared, or frustrated just before you start (or finish) that project. It could be that you're stuck in a job or relationship you've wanted to leave for years, but every time you get to that point, you hit your threshold and convince yourself to back away from the edge and find a way to be happy where you are. Maybe it's not one area but a general sense of incompletion—a work project not followed through on, a fix-it job that's half done, a conversation left hanging, a relationship riddled with unfinished moments. There's no judgment; just become aware of the patterns.

Notice the feelings that arise around these incomplete areas. As you start to identify these patterns and any commonality they may have, look for a core limiting belief that affects your whole life. Take a moment to contemplate this, meditate on it, and journal about it. Pose the questions:

- Where are my thresholds showing up?

- What are the core thoughts and emotions that come up for me right before I slow down, back away, or stop?

- What are the core thoughts and emotions I have around these areas now?

- What do I believe it means about myself when I don't complete something or back away from a challenge that's important to me? What's the self-talk? (I'm a loser, failure, inadequate, and so on.)

- What am I afraid will happen if do complete this project, go for this goal, have this conversation? (I'll fail, I'll make a fool of myself, be rejected, lose my job, and so on.)

- What am I afraid others will think of me if I complete this project, go for this goal, have this conversation? (I'm arrogant, selfish, greedy, controlling, and so on.)

As an example, if you left a relationship because you started feeling inadequate, invisible, or unappreciated, maybe you discover you're also struggling with those issues in your current relationship, making you want to leave. Then you recall that you left your last job or abandoned a creative venture because you felt something similar. As you scan your life, you see this same pattern has caused rifts in family, work, intimate relationships, or the pursuit of your deeper passions. It's always a familiar complaint: "They don't appreciate me. They're not seeing and validating me. They're not respecting me." Or in the case of a creative or entrepreneurial pursuit, it might sound like "Nobody will ever appreciate this. It's no good. I'm no good. This is a waste of time!" In other words, you take on the role of beating yourself up, since there's nobody else around to do it for you.

But it's still the same behavior—because it's still the same story.

At first, this kind of discovery may be unsettling. But take heart! This is the beginning of liberation. As you notice this repeating pattern, you begin to understand that nothing out there has ever been the problem; the problem has been these unconscious patterns. You know by now that you can't change other people, try as you might. What a relief to know you don't have to. You just have to change your inner pattern or your relationship to it. And *that* you can do. In fact, you're the only person who can. It's painful at first to realize that *you* are the common denominator in all your perceived failures, but it's also the beginning of true power.

When you look at these different situations through the lens of the work you've done in previous chapters, you become aware that any external triggers are irrelevant. The only thing that matters is what's *in you*. If you notice a pattern of feeling unappreciated, it's because you haven't activated this feeling of being appreciated within yourself. As you do so, using the practices in this book, *the quality of appreciation will become alive in you*. When it is, you'll either hold yourself so differently that others will appreciate you or you won't attract those who don't. You'll vibrate at a frequency that will drive unappreciative people away or you'll feel so supported from within that you won't care what people think at all.

Take a look at the answers to the questions above or any other insights you've had doing this process. Pay particular attention to the projections—the negative qualities you felt or feared others would think about you. These are your shadows. Notice which one resonates with you the strongest and then go back to the shadow work in Stage Six and work with it.

As I hope is becoming clear, a threshold is often an evolutionary catalyst and most problems are actually creating the conditions for answered prayer. Doing the work to get beyond a threshold brings you into a greater sense of self-love, appreciation, or whatever the seemingly missing quality was. Beyond the threshold, you're a new person. You've wrestled your angels, changed your nature, and moved up the ladder of consciousness. From this point, that relationship gets taken to the next stage, the work environment improves or expands, or that project gets completed and succeeds. Or if that person or place isn't able or willing to grow with you, you'll be moved into a relationship or environment that *can* play at this new level.

This is real change. Real evolution. You may still experience challenges in this area as you continue to grow, but you will *never cross that same threshold again.*

Getting Leverage on Your Life

You've been given the basic principles and practices to tap into your vision, create a plan, heal what's held you back, and stay on track—no matter what. You understand now that, just as an airplane can be off course 90 percent of the time, buffeted by the inertial forces, and still arrive at its destination on time, you, too, will be knocked off course as you travel the turbulent path of transformation. Like the plane, you have a destination—your vision—to give you direction, and a plan to direct your action. But this doesn't guarantee you'll keep moving toward it. Like the plane, you still need a system that notices when you're off track, makes an adjustment, and brings you back in line— or the natural drift will eventually land you far afield. The tools you've been given throughout this book will help you do this.

When you stay the course, no matter what, *you reach your destination.*

Sometimes we might get down on ourselves and want to stop or give up. We're up against a major threshold and we don't know it. Or we may know it but be too immobilized by fear or pain to do anything about it. That's when we need leverage, a support system, a strategy. This could mean joining a mastermind group, a group coaching program, having support partners, or even getting a private coach, mentor, or spiritual guide. Most great masters, leaders, artists, athletes, and entrepreneurs have some version of this. We all need help. This is not a solo flight; we're meant to take this journey together.

This leverage can take many forms. If you want to get in shape, it helps to have a workout buddy, making you more likely to show up when you don't feel like it. If you're trying to write or do some other creative project, find a creative partner you meet with weekly—in person or online—and work together. Having someone to hold you accountable will keep you on track and help you feel less lonely.

One client of mine, Valerie, wanted to write a certain number of pages per week but always found reasons not to get it done. So she made a deal with a friend that if she didn't reach her goal, she would take the friend out to an expensive meal. She couldn't afford many expensive meals, so she got the pages written. I've coached parents to make deals with their kids. The parent would meet a specific goal or they would clean their kids' rooms (or some other chore) for a week. You'd better believe those kids held their parents accountable!

Sometimes you can trick or ease yourself into it. Consider the following:

- If you want to start exercising, you might say to yourself, "All I have to do is go to the gym. I don't have to even work out. Just show up." Then you get there, fiddle around with a few machines, check out the people, and before you know it, you're working out.

- If you want to write or create something, you might tell yourself, "All I have to do is sit at my computer, open a word processor file, and type whatever comes to mind. It doesn't have to be good. I don't have to get it right, I just have to get *something* written." So you start typing your random thoughts, and—voilà—you're writing.

Emergineering isn't a magic recipe or get-rich-quick technique. There's no wishing, wondering, or hoping; you're engineering *a way of life* that supports you in being who you really are. Like the Chinese bamboo tree, it's about putting in the energy and having the patience to dig down and develop a root system that is deep, strong, and broad enough to support the great destiny you were born to live. As Henry David Thoreau said in *Walden*, "If one advances confidently in the direction of [one's] dreams, and endeavors to live the life which [one] has imagined, [then one] will meet with a success unexpected in common hours."[7]

LIVING ON THE
EMERGING EDGE

If you're not living on the edge, you're taking up too much space.

ANONYMOUS

It was born thousands of years before man built the first civilization along the river valleys of Mesopotamia. Even before the Great Pyramids rose from the Egyptian desert or the massive monoliths of Stonehenge were erected, this majestic being had already existed for millennia.

Its name is the Jurupa Oak. It first emerged through the soil during the last Ice Age and has since held its place like a great guardian of the ages atop a blustery hillside in southern California for well over thirteen thousand years, making it the oldest known living organism. Getting its name from the Jurupa Hills in Riverside County, this multimillennial oak extends over twenty-five yards and has learned to pace its growth to one twentieth of an inch per year, adding to its distinction as the most patient living organism in history and possibly making it much older than scientists think. It has ensured its survival through, among other things, developing a root system capable of drawing water and nourishment in a dry, rocky terrain, and re-sprouting directly from its roots after numerous wildfires.[1]

The Jurupa is a legacy tree, which is one that lives for generations, centuries, even millennia, and not only carries the past within it like some giant unwound scroll but also supports the future with all that it provides: food for some, shade for others, and a habitat for even more. A legacy tree preserves and protects nature and, as stated earlier, becomes a guardian of doors or the door itself—a door into the next season, because it waxes and wanes as the seasons do—or the gateway between earth and heaven, because it touches both the ground and sky.

The legacy tree's life is about more than its survival, more than its fulfillment. Its life belongs to the community it's planted in. It is often a centerpiece, a gathering place, or a beacon that draws people together, gathers them under its shade, and anchors them to the past, present, future—even to a sense of the eternal—in an enduring way.

Becoming a Legacy Tree

We've been taught that the ends we're seeking are about getting our body, business, mind, money, and relationships in shape. That's the initial function of the seven stages of Emergineering. But this is just the beginning. Once these life structures are stabilized through this work, they become planks in a platform that allows you to launch into your true destiny. If you're willing, you can use the principle of Emergence to live a life bigger than your personality, in service to a great vision, and become an instrument of evolutionary progress—in your family, your business, your community, and the world.

To do this, you must look more closely at your beliefs and actions, not just from the perspective of whether these work for you personally but also in regard to their impact on the planet, other people, and future generations. Do your behaviors, habits, and beliefs come from the evolutionary edge or are they artifacts of an old paradigm? As you discover your edge, you'll be able to release hidden blocks, expand your emerging potential, and live life as a visionary. Instead of living from the narrow paradigm of a human incarnation limited in time, you'll learn to live from your eternal nature, becoming a gateway between heaven and earth, and give roots to these timeless truths.

As you step into this next stage of your evolution, your actions, interests, and goals become increasingly about the impact they'll have not in one, five, or ten years but twenty-five, fifty, even a hundred years and beyond. As your sense of self begins to expand to include more of humanity and earth, the things that matter most and the projects you devote your life to become more about long-term sustainability, the evolution of the human race, and the future generations that will reap what you've sown. Your vision becomes not the end of the journey but a bold new beginning.

Kicking Old Habits

By this point, you've defined your vision and integrated the inner conflicts to establish a level of congruence that can bring that vision into expression, fully supported. You're serious about being the best version of yourself. To accelerate your progress, I invite you as you move forward to ask deeper questions about the way you live, questions that take you beyond personal fulfillment, questions that may challenge cherished beliefs or habits.

War is one example. But not war in the obvious sense. I'm referring to the less overt, but in some cases equally destructive, forms of war: the war on drugs, the war on poverty, the war on our bodies, and the war on ourselves. All war is within. It starts with a battle cry in our heart, a landmine exploding in our soul, firefights with parts of ourselves we deem dangerous, foreign invaders, and ultimately spills out into our world as all the conflicts we engage in: the family squabbles, the angry activism, the political partisanship, and the overall way we treat ourselves, each other, and the earth. We're waging wars on many fronts. But because what we resist persists and what we fight we fuel, *the more we wage war, the more we create something to fight against.*

So why is this important in activating the Law of Emergence more fully and living on your emerging edge? Am I just standing on a soapbox? No, this isn't about convincing you to think a certain way; it's about encouraging you *to think*. Most of what we do is not thinking; it's regurgitating old thoughts, many of which are not our own. True thinking is about using our mind as an avenue of awareness, opening it to the realm of the real, where the next stage of our evolution is always ready to emerge. In order to actualize our full potential, to become what we're meant to be, we must engage this evolutionary—even revolutionary—way of being.

Whether you choose to be or not, you're part of a larger system, like a branch on the legacy tree of life. And as it evolves, you must evolve with it or become obsolete. But you're also a whole system within yourself—your own legacy tree. As you do this work and become more refined in your energy use, you simultaneously transform those lower, denser ways of thinking, feeling, and behaving. As the vibration rises on the planet, those who want to rise with it will be supported and receive more energy if they're willing to let go of the lower energetic thoughts and habits, while those who aren't will receive less, until the amount of energy they receive is insufficient to support their continued Emergence.

As you live on the emerging edge, you're hitching a ride with the evolutionary power that is pulling the whole planet and cosmos forward—like drafting behind a semi—and you expand into your greater Self with ever more ease and grace. Your life begins to be driven by the universe instead of universal belief, and your capacity to be an instrument of good in the world is no longer based on your human abilities but on the limitlessness of life itself.

Finding Your Emerging Edge

The first part of this exercise can be done through journaling or with eyes closed, in which case you could record yourself speaking it and then play it back or have someone talk you through it. The second part is a timeline process, which is best done either with a friend, through a guided audio (as described above), or from memory after reading it over completely.

Start by taking a few cleansing breaths and set your intention with the basic prayer, "God (or whichever divine concept speaks to you personally), more than I want to control, manipulate, or change anything, I want to realize the truth that makes me free and makes me an instrument of the highest good for all." Feel the energy of that intention. You're not trying to get anything; you're opening to the truth of your being.

Ask your higher Self where you're holding on to an old way of doing or being, to an old paradigm or evolutionary perspective that's holding you back. Pay particular attention to any areas where you think to yourself, *I've always done it that way*. Maybe you learned a particular way of doing or being from your family, school, a job, or society as a whole. It might have worked for a while. It might still seem to work, but only in maintaining the status quo, not in allowing you to stretch and expand. You've outgrown it, mentally, emotionally, and energetically but haven't yet let go of it.

If you're struggling to grow in a particular area, ask yourself where, within that area or connected to it, you're trying to operate from an outmoded perspective or habit pattern, something no longer congruent with who you are or who you have been praying to become. What mental, emotional, or physical habits are in direct opposition to your higher vision or current prayers, affirmations, and heart's desires? For example, if you're praying to be more loving and understanding, when someone pushes your buttons, do you still defend, try to prove your point, or make them wrong? If it's abundance you're struggling with, do you complain about not having enough or how bad the economy is?

Be aware that the answer might be guarded by the ego in order to prevent you from changing in some inconvenient or uncomfortable way. You might have to give up gossiping, judging, or defending; you might have to forgive someone you resent, spend time alone instead of going out, meditate instead of watching television. Or it might be more challenging, like leaving a job or a relationship, or moving somewhere else.

These are powerful thresholds. A part of you has already arrived here, because of all the work you've done up to this point, but there is always room for further contemplation and evolution. Consider this "mastery work," as you release another layer of old habits and establish yourself more firmly on your emerging edge.

As you tune in to the mental, emotional, or physical habit you've identified as outdated or incongruent, ask how this pattern has served you. For example, has your defensiveness served as a shield between your ego and the world? Has your tendency to stay up too late on your computer kept you from confronting issues with insomnia or troubled sleep? In most cases, you'll find that these outmoded habits served you at some point or on some level. Don't think of them as wrong; just be willing to let them go so you can grow.

As you consider in what area you're clinging to outmoded beliefs, allow yourself to begin rising above it all, above your life, above your timeline (just as we did in Stage Six). From that vantage point, look down at the situation where you act in this particular way. Notice it without judgment. Appreciate it. Then imagine you've dropped the habit or adopted a new, more supportive one. Descend into the timeline and see yourself behaving this new way. See how it impacts your life. How do you treat yourself differently? How do you interact with others? What are you doing? Who are you being?

Rise back up and begin to move forward, noticing the timeline changing before your eyes, its colors becoming more vibrant, new possibilities joining it like tributaries. Without the old habits, your future is different. A whole new story is emerging. Keep moving forward—a month, two months, faster and faster, six months, a full year—and drop down into the timeline one year in the future, absent the old habit, having mastered the new. What do you see? What has changed? How do you feel? How are you behaving? Look at your life structures—relationships, work, finances, spirituality—and notice what, if anything, has changed. Have any new and unexpected treasures and treats emerged? If things look worse, if negative images arise, don't worry; that's a sign you've stirred unconscious material to the surface—some deeper roots have been struck. You can now go back and do the healing timeline process like we did before.

If you choose to go further, rise back up above your timeline and begin to float ahead . . . two years, three years, four years in the future. See the timeline zooming past beneath you. Feel the energy building. Feel the shifts and changes as this new habit continues to affect and impact every area of your life (for example, the cumulative effect of exercising regularly, not eating that particular food, no longer defending and complaining—whatever the new habit is—day after day, month after month, year after year). As you reach the five-year mark, drop down into the timeline and look around. What do you see now? What do you look like five years into the future of this new way of being? Who are you with? What are you doing? How are you impacting others? Again, if something negative appears, don't worry; you're shaking up old stuff. Make note of it and, if you're feeling pulled to go deeper, do the healing timeline process with it.

If you are satisfied with this new way of being, float back to the present moment and drop down into your body. Be grateful for the work you've done, for this cocreative moment with the evolutionary impulse of the universe. You've said yes to the yes within you. You're more congruent and more in alignment, and there's less resistance to your full nature that is emerging. Take a deep breath and relax into this knowing. You can return anytime to discover these evolutionary edges and move beyond them.

Living a Visionary Life

When Dr. Martin Luther King Jr. was gripped by a vision of racial equality, he had to release many ideas and habits to bring that vision into form and fulfill that role. He hadn't originally wanted to be a minister, and he didn't want to risk his safety or his family's. At one point, he lobbied to carry a concealed weapon and reportedly had an arsenal in his home (this from one of our greatest peace advocates). But as his calling deepened, he chose to model nonviolence and be more congruent with the teachings of Jesus. It wasn't easy; he had to live on the emerging edge. The same is true of Gandhi,

Mother Teresa, Oprah Winfrey, Thomas Jefferson, Thomas Edison, and Walt Disney. They all tapped a vision that forced them to release old concepts and leave their comfort zones in order to be congruent with the life trying to emerge as them.

Being a visionary is not about being famous or a history maker. You don't have to stand on a podium, carry a bullhorn, or march to the Capitol. It's about seeing things differently, seeing the invisible, and articulating it, whether to family, friends, colleagues, or the world. You can be a visionary parent, teacher, politician, artist, businessperson, or plumber. We're all called to live a visionary life, no matter what our station. It's about being true to the best in us. While others are following trends, judging by appearances, and being led like lemmings off the proverbial cliff, a visionary aligns their thoughts, words, and actions with the higher idea trying to emerge in them. They think for themselves, because if you're not thinking for yourself, someone else is thinking for you.

If you've caught a vision for your life or any aspect of it, you may already be moving in this direction. If not, return to Stage One and work with the vision process until it comes alive in you. Repeat this process as often as you want. Every time you use it, you're honing your soul-senses to see the invisible, hear the inaudible, and feel the intangible—so you can do the seemingly impossible.

This is the domain of the visionary. They see, hear, and sense the dimension of infinite potential and unbounded possibilities. This is where your true Self lives. This is where everything you could ever need to fulfill your destiny exists. This is the center all life emerges from. Just a word of warning: living from this place is not for the faint of heart. As Ralph Waldo Emerson said, "God will not have his work made manifest by cowards."[2]

The challenge of living a visionary life is that it's not always popular, because a visionary models, describes, and activates an

idea beyond the present paradigm, which will require something—
or someone—to change. This is what great leaders do, whether the
leader of a family, a community, a country, or a cause. By living as
an example and being an instrument of a higher ideal, they create
a kind of pressure in their environment that calls people to action.
Sometimes that pressure comforts the afflicted, but more often it
afflicts the comfortable, shaking up the status quo, uncovering the
places we're hiding, shining a light into our shadows, and cracking
open our protective shells when we're playing small.

Have you ever had the experience of being asleep in a dark room
and having someone suddenly throw open the curtains or turn on
the light? It's uncomfortable, and our impulse is to yell at the person
to shut off the light. Likewise, the part of us that lives in the dark
doesn't welcome the light; it burns our eyes. From the ego's perspective, it's dangerous, and the ego will attack, trying to shut it out or
shut it down. If you've been doing this work for some time, you've
probably had family, friends, or colleagues who have been less than
supportive of your ideas, dreams, and goals—maybe even judged,
shamed, or attacked you.

But while you might suffer some slings and arrows from those
not ready for your vision, you don't have to live a life of suffering or
martyr yourself. You don't need to convince people who aren't willing or interested or stand on a street corner with a sandwich board
over your shoulders prophesizing. You just need to stay the course,
forgive those who reject you, "shake the dust from your feet" and
walk on. Or as Jack Canfield put it in *The Aladdin Factor*, "SW SW
SW SW: Some will, some won't, so what—someone's waiting!"[3]

Your Life Is Not Your Own

Your life is not entirely your own. As we briefly explored at the start
of our journey, just as infinite forests are potential in every acorn,

your life plants seeds that will impact generations to come. The ways you think and act don't only expand or contract *your* life but also fertilize or deplete the soil of your environment—in your family, your profession, your community, and beyond. Every thought you think becomes part of the collective mind and potentially influences others in your life and throughout human consciousness. As a visionary, your higher vision acts as an antidote to the collective thought-viruses, planting itself in the hearts and minds of those you touch, working through their system, duplicating itself until it takes over. This is how you break the limiting legacies that have been handed down and, over time, transform not only your family but also entire cultures.

The inner and outer work you do, the words you say, and your impact in the world all make up the work of art called your life—your legacy. When you hear the name Jesus or Buddha, Shakespeare or da Vinci, Martin Luther King Jr. or Mother Teresa, you're not just hearing the name of a personality; you're sensing a vibration of eternity, a divine idea that has been made manifest through these beings. Beyond their great works, these individuals—and many more we've never heard of—caught a vision of life outside time and space, and then rooted it in human consciousness. This, more than anything, is what we feel when we connect to these individuals and their work—this is their legacy tree.

You have the same potential to tap into this eternal idea, this genius code within you, and ground it on earth in a way that will serve and bless your life, your family, and humanity for ages to come. Whether people ever know your name, if you do this work, the vibration of your life will continue to ripple through humanity forever because an eternal idea, once its Emergence is activated, has no end. Your life will become the seed that springs forth into infinite forests, an entire ecosystem that will serve and nourish many, long after you disappear from sight.

The One-Hundred-Year "Legacy" Vision

One way to anchor yourself in this larger vision is to contemplate the impact of your life over many generations. I call it the One-Hundred-Year Legacy Vision. It can be fun and liberating to think about your life this way.

Let's take a moment to tap into it.

Allow yourself to become still. Take a few deep breaths into your heart and relax. When you're ready, ask yourself the following questions:

- What is the impact of my highest vision one hundred years in the future?

- If I lived my divine purpose, what would the impact be on my family in one hundred years?

- If I lived my divine purpose, how could it impact my industry in one hundred years?

- If I lived my divine purpose, how would it impact my country in one hundred years?

- If I lived my divine purpose, how would it impact the planet in one hundred years?

If you're feeling bold, expand this further and ask, "If I lived my vision fully, what would its impact be in a *thousand* years?" One act of loving-kindness today can have a ripple effect that circles the globe. That smile you give someone on the bus could save a person's life. Maybe they were in a horrible mood, but because of that act of care, they don't fight with their wife tonight. Maybe if they had fought, it would have ended in divorce. But this night, it ends in making love, and a child is conceived. That child grows up and discovers a cure for some disease or becomes a firefighter who saves someone from a burning building, and that person they saved goes on to do something important for another—or for the world. On and on the impact goes, for years, decades, centuries, changing countless lives in a never-ending upward spiral.

The actions of one moment can indeed change the world.

If one conscious moment could have that kind of impact, imagine the impact an entire life lived fully could have—thousands of moments rippling across time, touching innumerable lives, activating unimaginable potential, cultivating the emergence of whole new ways of living and whole new worlds of possibility. Can you see that? Can you feel it? Sense the power you have. Take a deep breath and draw that power back into you in this moment. All that ability to heal lives, transform industry, and change the planet—all that confidence, genius, love, and wisdom is in you right now. Just as infinite forests already exist in the acorn, this infinity of power is in you now.

As you expand the bounds of your imagination, letting it break free from the limits of time and space, and tap into new avenues of insight and possibility, ask:

- What is the highest vision for my life? What is trying to emerge in my life? What idea does God (or whichever divine concept you resonate with most) have for my life?

- How must I change? What must I release, embrace, let go of, or become to create the right conditions for my highest vision to unfold in this lifetime?

- How must I change or what must I release or embrace to allow for my One-Hundred-Year Legacy Vision to unfold?

- Who do I need to become now in order to ensure that the One-Hundred-Year Legacy Vision happens?

- What action(s) am I being called to take to step into the reality of this vision, to lean into the highest possibility of my life?

The answers to some of these questions may be beyond what you can intellectually envision, but the timeless soul will know. Through the soul, you have access to a reservoir of potential you may have never tapped into. As a vision emerges, let the fullness of it wash through you. Don't judge or edit anything that comes up. Maybe you see its impact on your children, their children, and their children's children. Maybe you realize that something you're doing now could lead to your grandchildren growing up and making a significant change or hinder them if you don't stop a particular activity.

You start to see that what you may have deemed insignificant or small compared to other worldly visions is part of a much larger purpose. Stretched to these lengths, your life impact is as important as the greatest person who ever lived. Rather than walking around with the small vibration of what you perceive as your meager human history, you carry the energy of the whole human purpose—and begin to express that cosmic force in every step.

The Greatest Calling

One of the great shifts of the Emergence model is a move from merely self-fulfillment to service. We are here to plant trees whose fruit will ripen for future generations. As we've been discovering, our life is not really our own, and we're not here just for us. As we realize we already have everything and are part of a system of *one*, our life becomes about helping others awaken to their full potential. It becomes the reason we wake up, the fuel that powers us through the dark nights. We live to give and make a contribution wherever we go. Conflict and competition dissolve in the realization that we are one. As the Ojibwa saying goes: "No tree has branches so foolish as to fight amongst themselves."[4]

This is about becoming a servant of life, whether on the world stage or in your community or family, where you become an instrument of not only your own Emergence but many others' Emergence as well. Everyone is called to this, but few answer the call. If you've made it this far, practiced this material, and stayed the course, you're one of the few.

So congratulations. And thank you. As your consciousness is elevated, it raises all of human consciousness. And when enough of us lift our vibration to a higher level, others begin to spontaneously awaken.

In one of many studies on the impact of raising consciousness, a group of approximately four thousand meditators from the transcendental meditation program of Maharishi Mahesh Yogi went to Washington, DC, and meditated for two months in an experiment to see if creating greater group coherence and reducing stress in the collective consciousness could reduce crime. Their hypothesis proved correct. During that period, the crime rate *did* drop by up to twenty-three percent. Every time you meditate, lift your consciousness, or have a breakthrough, you become like the leaven in the bread that allows others to rise.[5]

This is the deeper role of the Emergineer. It's not just about engineering the Emergence of your life but the Emergence of the planet. This is the highest form of service, the true meaning of greatness. As Martin Luther King, Jr. said, "Everybody can be great because anybody can serve."[6]

The Ongoing Journey of Emergence

Along this journey of Emergence, you've probably had many insights, made many shifts, and committed or recommitted to a bold vision. You may have also run into many obstacles and unearthed core fears and limited beliefs, stretching yourself in ways that weren't always comfortable. Just know that whatever has come up, it's all good and all part of the normal process of growth. In other words, wherever you are today is exactly where you should be.

You know how I know?

Because it's where you are, it couldn't be any other way.

Be patient and kind to yourself, treat yourself the way you would want others to treat you. Even better, treat yourself the way you would treat a person you deeply cherish.

Every day.

This is a never-ending, ever-expanding adventure. There's no finish line and it's not a race. You're an infinite being on a path of endless Emergence. No matter how much has unfolded, there is always more waiting to break through the surface. Appreciate where you are, where you've been, and what you've accomplished.

Keep digging your roots deeper, stretching your branches further, lifting your oak heart higher toward the sun—and blessing all who gather beneath the shade of your legacy tree.

To your Emergence!

ACKNOWLEDGMENTS

The more you understand the true nature of life, the more you realize that the whole universe has conspired to make each moment possible. In that light, I am thankful for everyone and everything that has led to the emergence of this book.

Specific individuals have been guiding lights, helping hands, and healing agents on my path, without whom I probably wouldn't be here, let alone have written this book. Thank you to my mom, who always believed in me, even when I didn't believe in myself; her faith gave me wings. My dad, who brought me back down to earth; his practical wisdom grounded me in the world. My wife, who has been my greatest champion and critic, shadow dancing with me so I could see where my heart needed to grow. (Still working on it, babe!) My kids, who help me keep it real; I thought I had so much to teach them, but when the student is *really* ready, the children appear to teach!

My deep thanks to Michael Bernard Beckwith, who not only brought this prodigal son home to God and anchored me in the universal principles of truth but activated a hunger to awaken, which has only grown stronger. And to Nirvana Gayle, a spiritual mentor who sat with me and prayed with me, helping a young lost boy integrate these teachings and become a confident man. In many ways, this book is the offspring of both these great souls.

I'm grateful for Joel Goldsmith, a powerful mystic and healer who left this world before I got here but whose teachings have been a constant source of inspiration and renewal, challenging me to live with an ever-deeper spiritual integrity. Then there's Jesus, with whom my relationship is anything but typical. As a teacher of universal truth and a student of the world's great religions and philosophies, I respect all spiritual masters, from Buddha to Yoda. I am richly fed by their wisdom. But for some reason, the teachings of this rabbi from Galilee have grown to be the bread and water that nourish me the deepest.

This book could never have happened if it weren't for the faith, patience, and tenacity of my agent, Stephany Evans, who believed in this work through thick and thin, guiding it—and me—every step of the way. Thank you, Anna Noak, my editor, who not only believed in this book but also believed I was a better writer than I knew. She never took "good enough" for an answer! Her willingness to go toe-to-toe with me not only made this a better book but also made me a better writer, and maybe even a better person. Thanks to Gretchen Stelter, Sylvia Spratt, Sheila Ashdown, and Lindsay Brown, who also tirelessly edited this manuscript, not to mention put up with my rambling questions and comments in the margins. You're all editing goddesses, and I'm deeply grateful for your efforts.

There are many others at Beyond Words, Atria, and Simon & Schuster who have worked hard to make this book a reality and who continue to do so long after its release. To all of you, please know how thankful I am for your contribution.

And, finally, at the risk of sounding cliché, I thank God in all its forms for breathing its spirit into my soul, into this book, and into this world. We've got a pretty good thing going here. My prayer is that this work can, in some way, make life a little better for all.

NOTES

Biblical quotes are from numerous sources, including *English Standard Version Bible* © 2009 by Oxford University Press; *New American Standard Bible* © 1997 by Foundation Publications; *Holy Bible, King James Bible* © 2009 by Thomas Nelson, HarperCollins Christian Publishing; *New International Version Bible* © 2001 by Zondervan.

Preface

1. Alison King, "From Sage on the Stage to Guide on the Side," *College Teaching* 41, no. 1 (Winter 1993): 30–35, http://www.jstor.org/stable/27558571.

Introduction

1. Colin Tudge, *The Tree: A Natural History of What Trees Are, How They Live and Why They Matter* (New York: Three Rivers Press, 2006), 193–195.

2. William Bryant Logan, *Oak: The Frame of Civilization* (New York: W. W. Norton, 2005), 30–32.

3. Ibid., 90–95.

4. Michael Bernard Beckwith, *Your Life's Purpose: Life Visioning Practices for Activating Your Highest Potential* (Louisville, CO: Sounds True, 2012), compact disc.

5. US Department of Health and Human Services, Centers for Disease Control and Prevention, National Center for Health Statistics, National Vital Statistics System, *National Vital Statistics Report* 58, no. 19 (May 2010): table 29, http://www.cdc.gov/nchs/data/nvsr/nvsr58/nvsr58_19.pdf; Federal Bureau of Investigation Uniform Crime Report, Expanded Homicide Data (2007): table 20, http://www2.fbi.gov/ucr/cius2007/data/table_20.html.

6. Helen Schucman, *A Course in Miracles* (New York: Viking, Foundation for Inner Peace, 2007), 88.

Foundation

1. Hermes Trismegistus, *Hermetica: The Greek Corpus Hermeticum and the Latin Asclepius in a New English Translation, with Notes and Introduction*, ed. Brian P. Copenhaver (Cambridge University Press, 1995). Goodreads, http://www.goodreads.com/quotes/636262-as-above-so-below-as-within-so-without-originated-by. Originally recorded in the Kybalion, a hermetic text published anonymously in 1908.

2. Michael Talbot, *The Holographic Universe: The Revolutionary Theory of Reality* (New York: Harper Perennial, 1991).

3. Elizabeth Knowles, ed., *Oxford Dictionary of Quotations*, 7th ed. (New York: Oxford University Press, 2009), 119.

4. Walter Isaacson, *Einstein: His Life and Universe* (New York: Simon & Schuster, 2008), 20.

5. James Hillman, *The Soul's Code: In Search of Character and Calling* (New York: Grand Central Publishing, 1997).

6. Masaki Kobayashi, Daisuke Kikuchi, and Hitoshi Okamura, "Imaging of Ultraweak Spontaneous Photon Emission from Human Body Displaying Diurnal Rhythm," *PLOS ONE* 4, no. 7 (2009), doi:10.1371/journal.pone.0006256.

7. William Ernest Henley quotes, ThinkExist.com, http://en.thinkexist.com/quotation/it_matters_not_how_strait_the_gate-how_charged/158349.html.

8. Pierre Teilhard de Chardin, Goodreads, http://www.goodreads.com/quotes/21263-we-are-not-human-beings-having-a-spiritual-experience-we.

9. "Distant Healing Studies and Articles, Research Studies," IONS: Institute of Noetic Sciences, http://www.noetic.org/research/project/compassionat-inten tion-prayer-and-distant-healing/reading/; Larry Dossey, "A Conversation About the Future of Medicine," http://www.dosseydossey.com/larry/QnA.html; Larry Dossey, "Prayer and Medical Science," Archives of Internal Medicine, (June 26, 2000) 160: 1735–1738, http://www.mercola.com/article/prayer/dossey .htm.

10. Ralph Waldo Emerson quote, ThinkExist.com, http://thinkexist.com/quotation /the_dice_of_god_are_always_loaded/297304.html.

11. Helen Schucman, *A Course in Miracles* (New York: Viking, Foundation for Inner Peace, 2007), 303.

Stage One

1. Albert Einstein quote, ThinkExist.com, http://thinkexist.com/quotation/imagi nation_is_more_important_than_knowledge-for/260230.html.

Stage Three

1. George T. Doran, "There's a S.M.A.R.T. Way to Write Management's Goals and Objectives," *Management Review* 70.11 (Nov. 1981): 35, EBSCO Business Source Corporate.

2. Pelé (Edson Arantes do Nscimento) quote, ThinkExist.com, http://thinkexist .com/quotation/everything-is-practice/535485.html.

3. Jennifer White, *Work Less, Make More: Stop Working So Hard and Create the Life You Really Want!* (Hoboken, NJ: John Wiley & Sons, 1999), 75.

Stage Five

1. D. H. S Nicholson and A. H. E. Lee, eds., *The Oxford Book of English Mystical Verse* (Oxford: Clarendon Press, 1917); Bartleby.com (2000), http://www.bartleby .com/236/102.html.

2. Franz Kafta quote, Goodreads, http://www.goodreads.com/quotes/18883-you -do-not-need-to-leave-your-room-remain-sitting.

3. Kurt Vonnegut, *Mother Night* (Robbinsdale, MN: Fawcett, 1961).

4. Mahatma Gandhi quote, ThinkExist.com, http://thinkexist.com/quotation/to _believe_in_something-and_not_to_live_it-is/216405.html.

5. Wayne Gretzky quote, BrainyQuote.com, http://www.brainyquote.com/quotes /quotes/w/waynegretz383282.html.

6. Ralph Waldo Emerson quote, ThinkExist.com, http://thinkexist.com/quotation /do_the_thing_and_you_will_be_given_the/167062.html.

7. Bhagavad Gita quote, ThinkExist.com, http://thinkexist.com/quotation/those _who_consciousness_is_unified_abandon_all/254220.html.

8. Bhagavad Gita, 4:18, KrishnaStore.org, http://prabhupadabooks.com/bg/4/18.

9. Franklin D. Roosevelt quotes (date unknown), http://aboutfranklindroosevelt. com/franklin-delano-roosevelt-quotes/480/.

10. Edward Everett Hale quote, BrainyQuote.com, http://www.brainyquote.com /quotes/quotes/e/edwardever393297.html. Edward Everett Hale was a one-time chaplain of the United States Senate but was best known for his novel, *The Man without a Country*.

11. Oliver Wendell Holmes quote, BrainyQuote.com, http://www.brainyquote.com /quotes/quotes/o/oliverwend392895.html.

Stage Six

1. Vanessa Chiasson, "Discovering 'The Jack Pine' in Algonquin Provincial Park," *Ontario Travel Blog*, December 9, 2013, http://ontariotravelblog.com/2013 /12/09/discovering-the-jack-pine-in-algonquin-provincial-park/.

2. Brian Tracy, *Change Your Thinking, Change Your Life: How to Unlock Your Full Potential for Success and Achievement* (Hoboken, NJ: John Wiley & Sons, 2005), 189.

3. Jesus Christ quotes, ThinkExist.com, http://thinkexist.com/quotation/if-you -bring-forth-what-is-within-you-what-you/1329600.html. Part of the New Testament, Apocrypha, or lost books of the Bible are not included in the final canonized version.

4. William Shakespeare quote, BrainyQuote.com, http://www.brainyquote.com /quotes/quotes/w/williamsha166828.html.

5. Greg Botelho, Vivian Kuo, and Josh Levs, "Antoinette Tuff Hailed as 'True Hero' for Handling Georgia School Gunman," CNN online, August 22, 2013, http ://www.cnn.com/2013/08/21/us/georgia-school-gunshots/.

6. Mark Memmott, "Only 'A Good Guy with a Gun' Can Stop School Shootings, NRA Says." *The Two-Way* (blog), National Public Radio, December 21, 2012, http://www.npr.org/blogs/thetwo-way/2012/12/21/167785169/live-blog-nra -news-conference/.

7. Debbie Ford, *The Dark Side of the Light Chasers: Reclaiming Your Power, Creativity, Brilliance, and Dreams* (New York: Riverhead Books, 2010).

Stage Seven

1. "Fastest Growing Plant," Guinness World Records, http://www.guinnessworld records.com/records-3000/fastest-growing-plant/.

2. Helen Schucman, "Healing and Wholeness," *A Course in Miracles* (New York: Viking, Foundation for Inner Peace, 2007).

3. Russell H. Conwell, *Acres of Diamonds*, (1869; Project Gutenberg, 2008), http:// www.gutenberg.org/files/368/368-h/368-h.htm/.

4. Samuel Johnson quote, BrainyQuote.com, http://www.brainyquote.com/quotes /quotes/s/samueljohn385293.html.

5. Lucinda Vardey, *Mother Teresa: A Simple Path* (New York: Ballantine Books, 1995), 185.

6. Eckhart Tolle, *A New Earth: Awaken to Your Life's Purpose* (New York: Penguin, 2005), 87.

7. Henry David Thoreau, *Walden* (Seattle: CreateSpace Independent Publishing Platform, 2014), 181.

Living on the Emerging Edge

1. Steve Connor, "At 13,000 Years, Tree Is World's Oldest Organism," *Independent*, December 22, 2009, http://www.knowtex.com/nav/at-13-000-years-tree-is -world-s-oldest-organism_5943.

2. Ralph Waldo Emerson, *Self-Reliance and Other Essays* (Seattle: CreateSpace Independent Publishing Platform, 2014), 2.

3. Jack Canfield, *The Aladdin Factor* (New York: Berkley, 2002).

4. Ojibwa quote, Illustrated World of Proverbs, http://www.worldofproverbs .com/2012/12/no-tree-has-branches-so-foolish-as-to.html.

5. J. S. Hagelin et al., "Effects of Group Practice of the Transcendental Meditation Program on Preventing Violent Crime in Washington, D.C.: Results of the National Demonstration Project, June–July, 1993," *Social Indicators Research* 47, no. 2 (1999): 153–201.

6. Martin Luther King Jr. quote, ThinkExist.com, http://thinkexist.com/quotation /everybody_can_be_great_because_anybody_can_serve/9180.html.

GLOSSARY

desire path: a footpath worn thin by travelers as they find the best route to a desired place (also called a desire line).

Emergineering: the process of enacting the seven stages of Emergence in one's life.

Emergination: a faculty of the soul that allows it to tap into the divine blueprint behind all form, the original forms (also referred to as Imagination 2.0).

feeling tone: where emotions are energy in motion or the transmutation of thought in the emotional body, a feeling tone is the energy of the soul, the true essence or frequency of our being. Whereas emotions will change and eventually dissipate with mindful awareness, a feeling tone—because it's real, unchanging, and infinite—will continue to expand and increase in intensity with focused attention.

LIFT: Stands for Living In the Feeling Tone of your vision, aka your visionary vibration. The Daily LIFT is part of the three steps to congruent conditions in Stage Two: Cultivate Congruent Conditions.

quantum plan: a plan that is focused on creating a life structure that mirrors its soul's blueprint (our divine *desire path*) and supports its emergence. It is not a plan that is about simply achieving. In physics, the word "quantum" refers to the minimum amount of any physical entity involved in an interaction. In quantum mechanics, "quantum" is used to describe the fundamental framework for understanding nature at its most essential. In short, it is our core essence in action. We align with this core and plan from that level, and arrive at our destination before we take the first step. A quantum plan is more concerned with *who* is trying to emerge than with *what* is externally accomplished. It's designed to accelerate your evolution, to pull more of the real you out. If the end goal of your plan doesn't require you to change, to become more of yourself, it's not a quantum plan; it's just a plan. It must bring more of your infinite potential to the surface.

Soul Purpose Pillars: feeling, being, and doing. Part of the three steps to congruent conditions in Stage Two: Cultivate Congruent Conditions.

soul-sense: whereas taste, touch, sight and sound are perceptual faculties of the body, a soul-sense is an inner perceptual faculty that allows us to see and feel inner realms beyond the material senses.

Vision Statement: a present-tense affirmation that describes the actualization of a vision as if it has already happened or is happening. Usually written down for daily repetition.

Vision Studio: a sacred inner environment you create to discover, define, and design your ideal vision, where the editor, critic, and analyst aren't allowed—at least not until you've expressed a complete version of your vision that inspires you.

The key to creating this creative sanctuary is a willingness to stay in an open, nonjudgmental, childlike space.

visionary vibration: the unique energetic signature of your vision; how you feel when you imagine living it. More than just a good feeling, this is the very essence and substance of your emerging vision.

RESOURCES

Visit my site, **www.DerekRydall.com**, to learn about my work, events, and other free tools, including the suggested direct resources below:

Free tools to support your Emergence
www.derekrydall.com/main/free-offers/

The VVR audio process that is part of the LIFT practice in the book
www.derekrydall.com/vibrationradiation/

Get a month of private group coaching with Derek Rydall (along with a lot of other resources for just a penny)
http://www.derekrydall.com/bestyearofyourlife

A free audio eCourse to support growth
www.LawOfEmergence.com

A free audio e-course on the Shadow Process found in Stage Six
www.derekrydall.com/shadowprocess